**AA** ATLAS BRITAIN

# Contents

| | |
|---|---|
| Map pages | II |
| Atlas symbols | 1 |
| **Road maps of Britain 1:500,000 scale** | **2–65** |
| Index to place names in Britain | 66–80 |
|     County, administrative area map | 66–67 |
|     Place name index | 68–80 |
| **Distance charts** | **81 & 90** |
|     Britain | 81 |
|     Ireland | 90 |
| **Road maps of Ireland 1:1 million scale** | **82–89** |
| Index to place names in Ireland | 91–94 |
|     County, administrative area map | 91 |
|     Place name index | 92–94 |

16th edition July 2017

© AA Media Limited 2017

**Cartography:**
All cartography in this atlas edited, designed and produced by the Mapping Services Department of AA Publishing (A05536).

This atlas contains Ordnance Survey data © Crown copyright and database right 2017 and data from openstreetmap.org © OpenStreetMap Contributors (pages 82–94 only)

**Publisher's notes:**
Published by AA Publishing (a trading name of AA Media Limited, whose registered office is Fanum House, Basing View, Basingstoke, Hampshire RG21 4EA, UK. Registered number 06112600).

ISBN: 978 0 7495 7880 0 (paperback)

ISBN: 978 0 7495 7879 4 (wire bound)

A CIP Catalogue record for this book is available from the British Library.

**Disclaimer:**
The contents of this atlas are believed to be correct at the time of the latest revision, it will not contain any subsequent amended, new or temporary information including diversions and traffic control or enforcement systems. The publishers cannot be held responsible or liable for any loss or damage occasioned to any person acting or refraining from action as a result of any use or reliance on material in this atlas, nor for any errors, omissions or changes in such material. This does not affect your statutory rights.

The publishers would welcome information to correct any errors or omissions and to keep this atlas up to date. Please write to the Atlas Editor, AA Publishing, The Automobile Association, Fanum House, Basing View, Basingstoke, Hampshire RG21 4EA, UK.
E-mail: *roadatlasfeedback@theaa.com*

**Printer:** 1010 Printing International Ltd.

Scale 1:500,000
or 8 miles to 1 inch
5km to 1cm

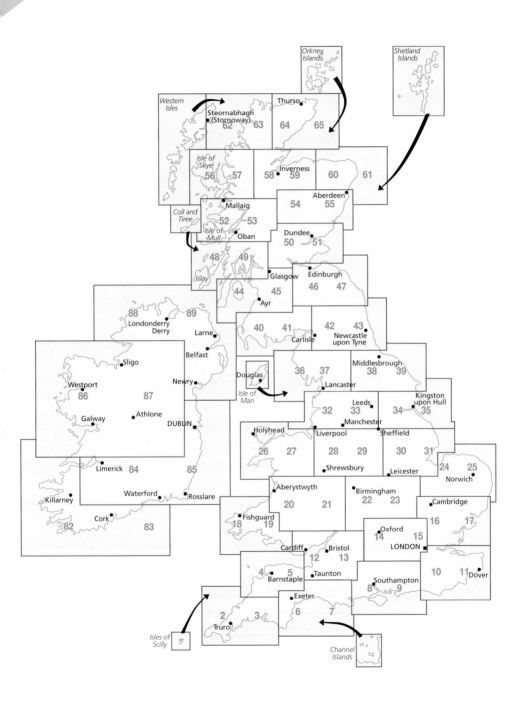

# Britain

|  |  |
|---|---|
| M4 | Motorway with number |
| Toll T4 | Toll motorway with junction |
| 40 | Motorway junction with and without number |
| 40 | Restricted motorway junction |
| Fleet S | Motorway service area |
| A40 | Primary route single/dual carriageway |
| | Primary route junction with and without number |
| 4 | Restricted primary route junction |
| S | Primary route service area |
| A33 | Other A road single/dual carriageway |
| B4224 | B road |
| | Unclassified road |
| | Road tunnel |
| | Road under construction/approved |

Narrow primary, other A or B road with passing places (Scotland)

Toll — Road toll

5 — Distance in miles between symbols

or V — Vehicle ferry

Fast vehicle ferry or catamaran

National boundary

County, administrative boundary

(H) Heliport

(✈) Airport

Viewpoint

931 ▲ SKIDDAW — Spot height in metres

National Park or National Scenic Area

27 — Page overlap with number

**1:500,000** 0 5 10 miles / 0 5 10 15 kilometres

8 miles to 1 inch

# Ireland

|  |  |
|---|---|
| M1 | Motorway |
| M1 Toll | Toll motorway and plaza |
| 3 | Motorway junction with and without number |
| 3 | Restricted motorway junction with and without number |
| Gorey S | Motorway service area |
| N7 | National primary route (Republic of Ireland) |
| N81 | National secondary route (Republic of Ireland) |
| R116 | Regional road (Republic of Ireland) |
| 7 | Distance in kilometres between symbols (Republic of Ireland) |
| A2 | Primary route (Northern Ireland) |
| A42 | A road (Northern Ireland) |
| B176 | B road (Northern Ireland) |

7 — Distance in miles between symbols (Northern Ireland)

Minor road

Road tunnel

Road under construction

or V — Vehicle ferry

Fast vehicle ferry or catamaran

International boundary

(✈) Airport

Viewpoint

919 ▲ Galtymore — Spot height in metres

Gaeltacht (Irish language area)

**1:1,000,000** 0 10 20 miles / 0 10 20 30 kilometres

16 miles to 1 inch

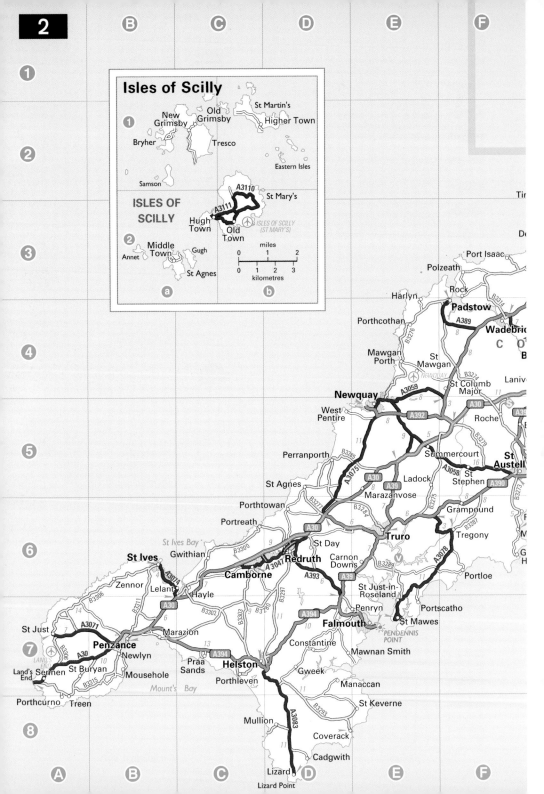

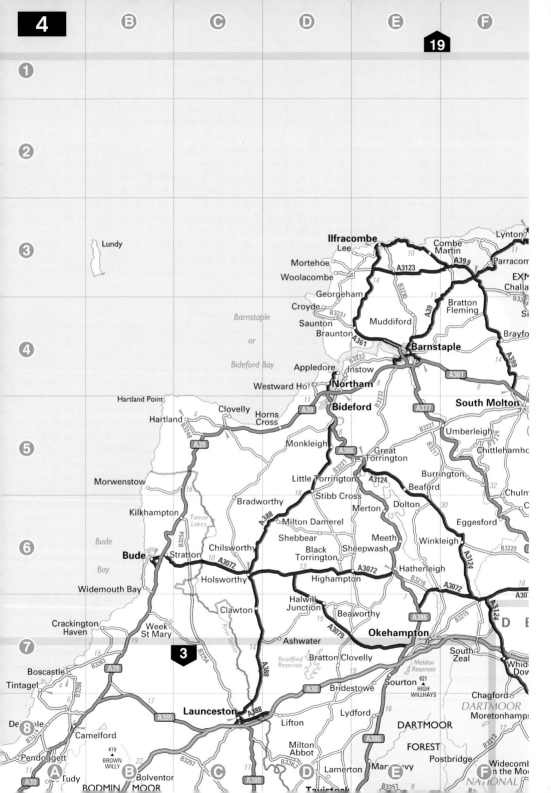

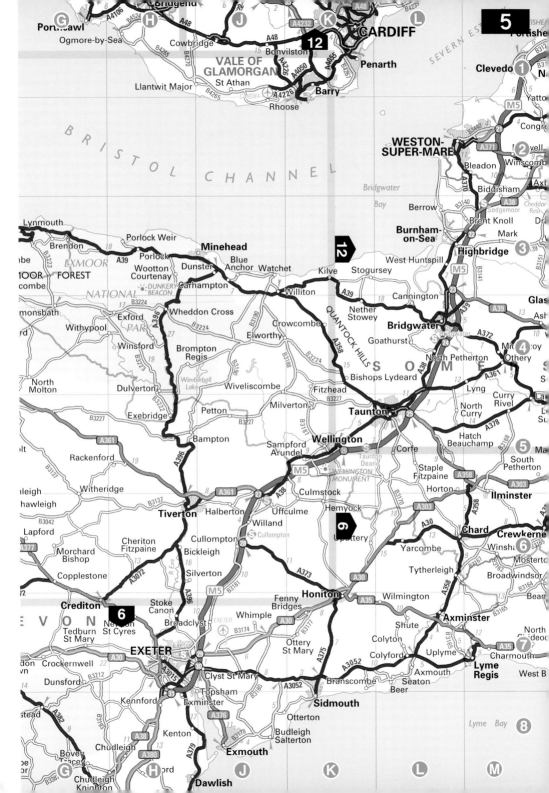

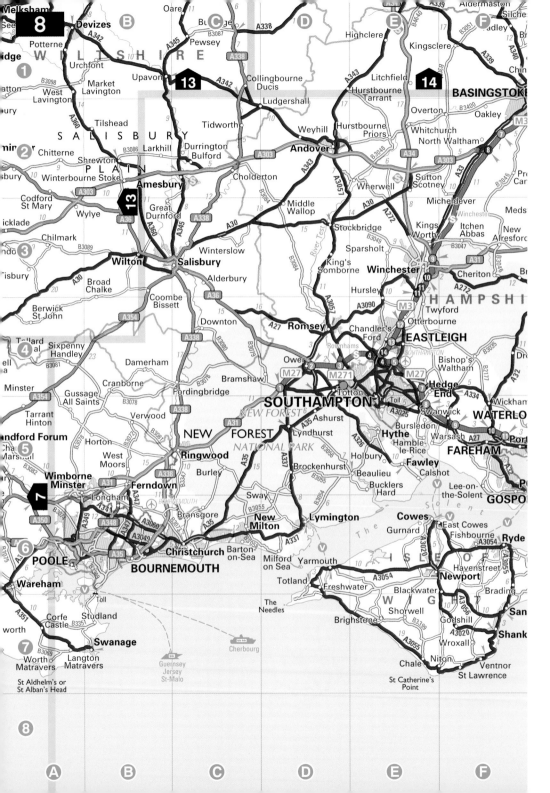

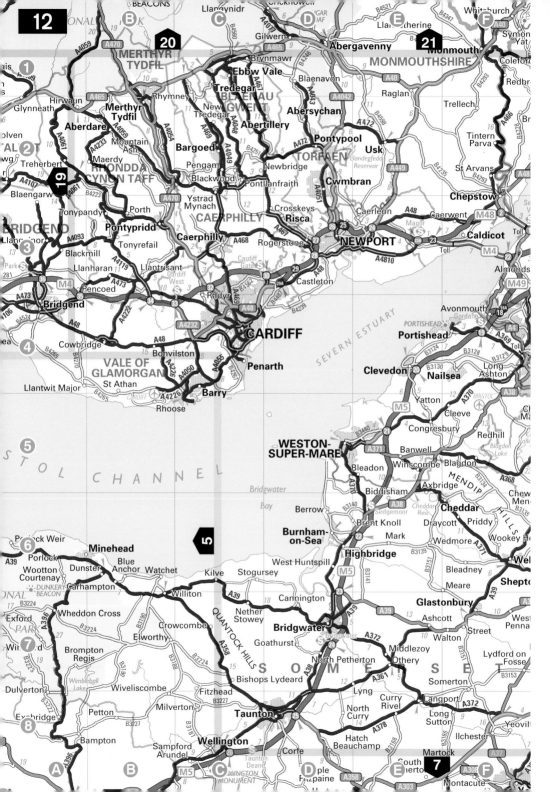

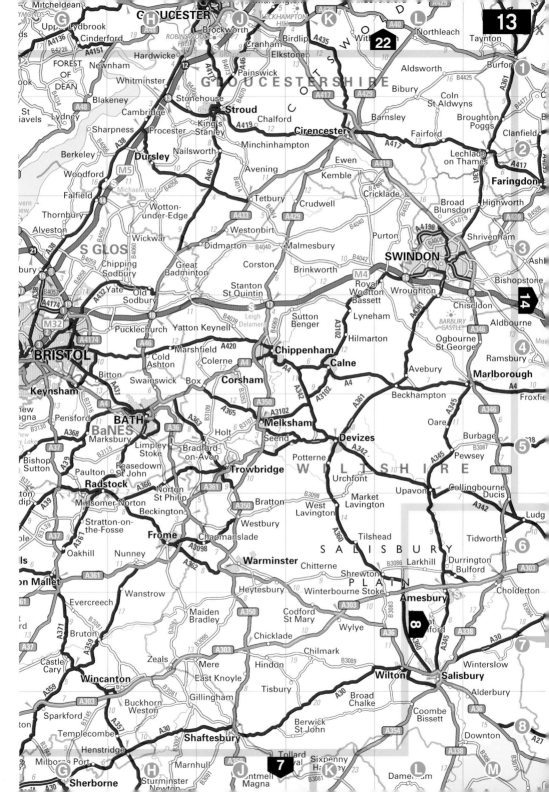

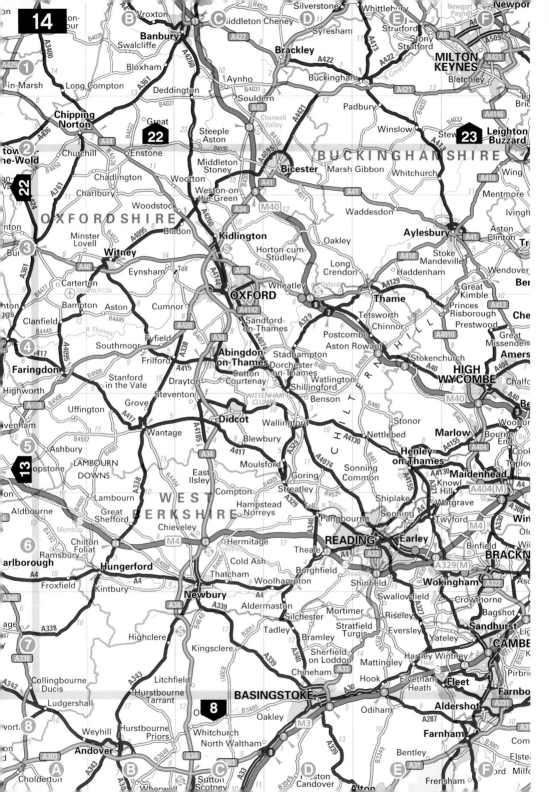

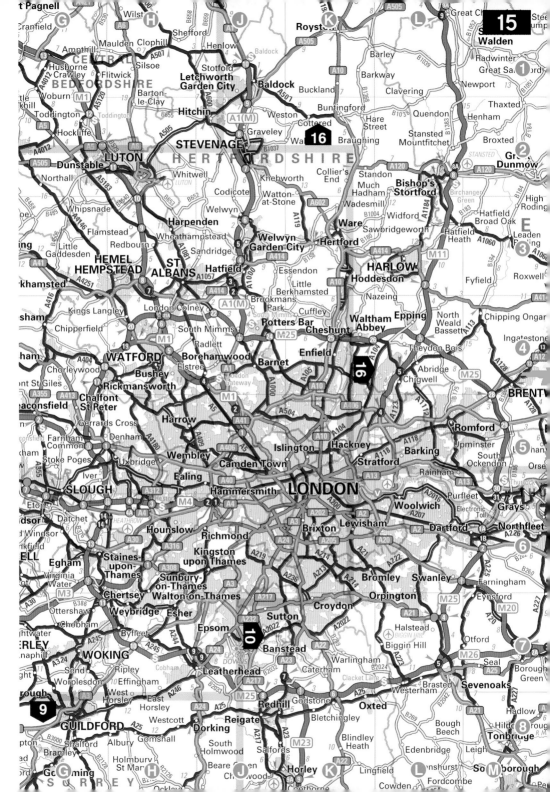

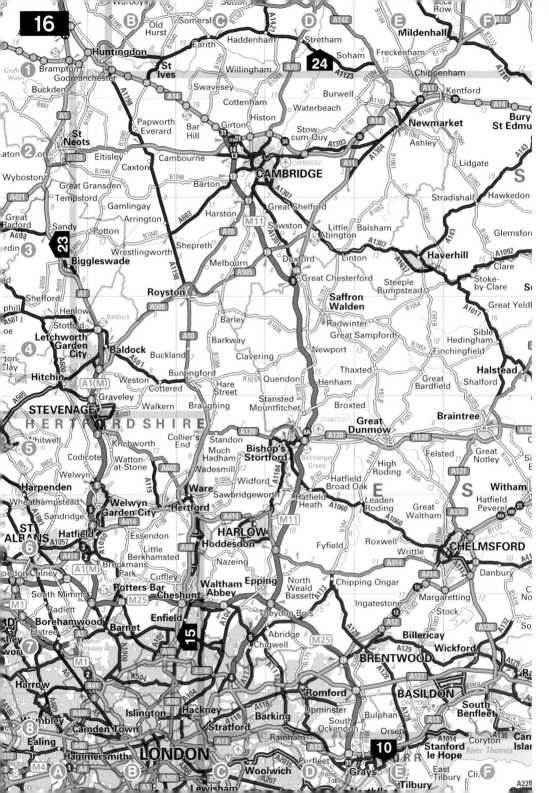

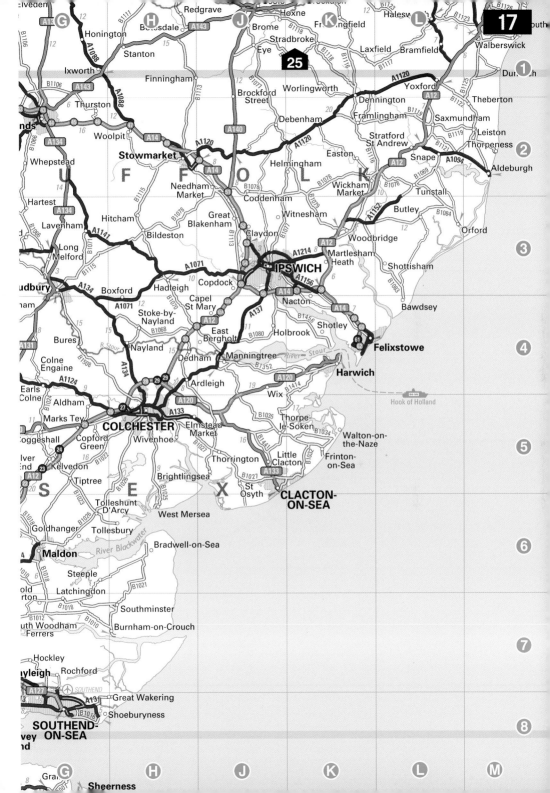

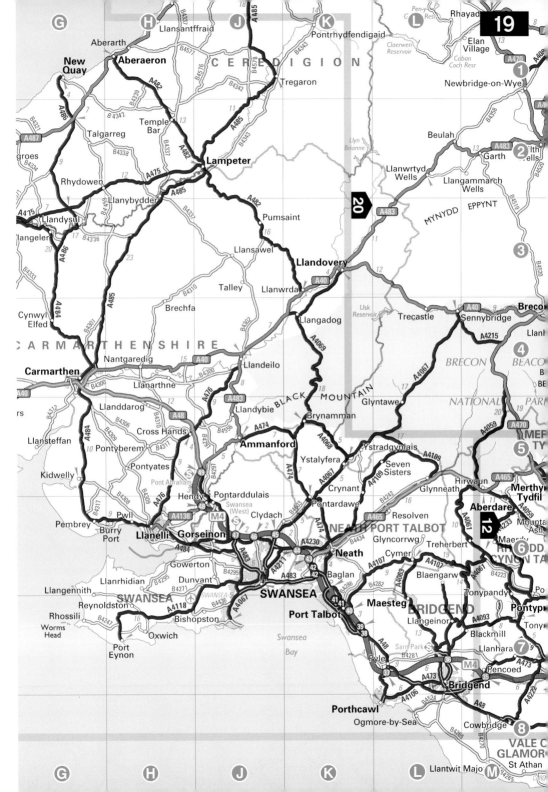

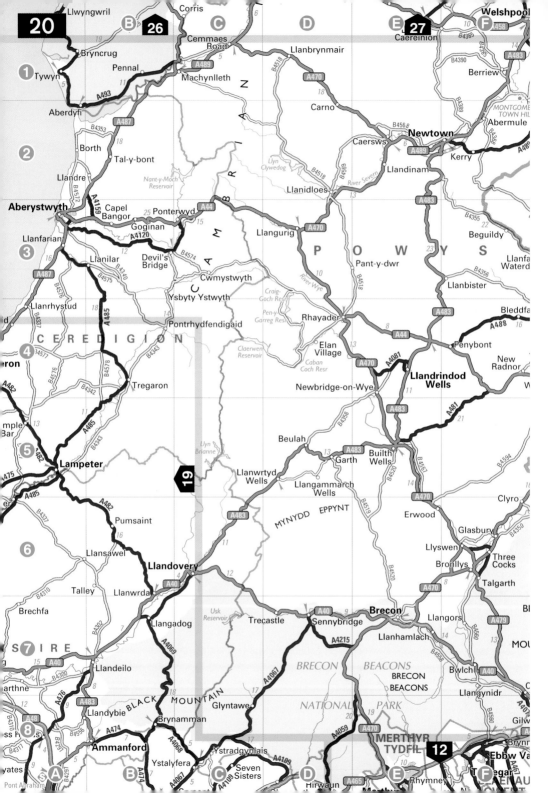

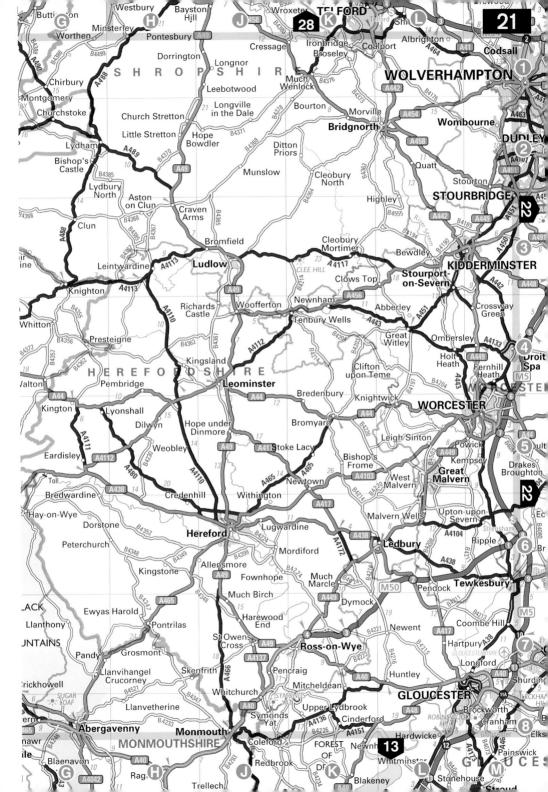

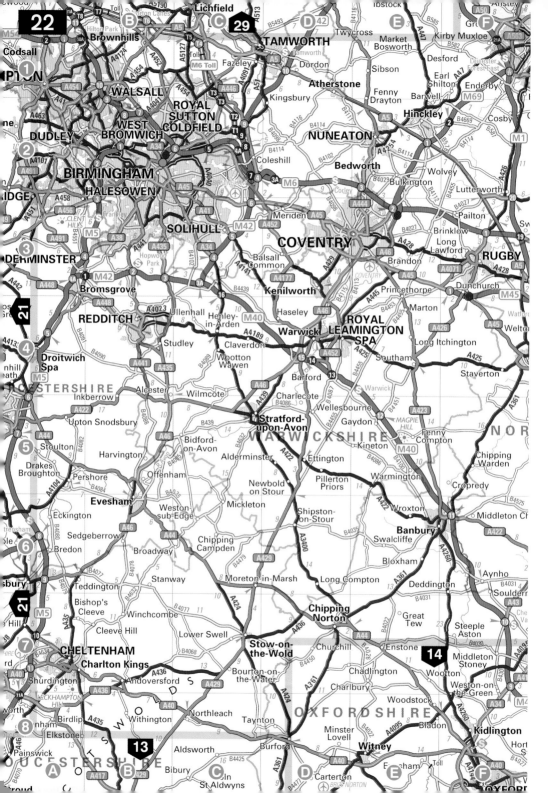

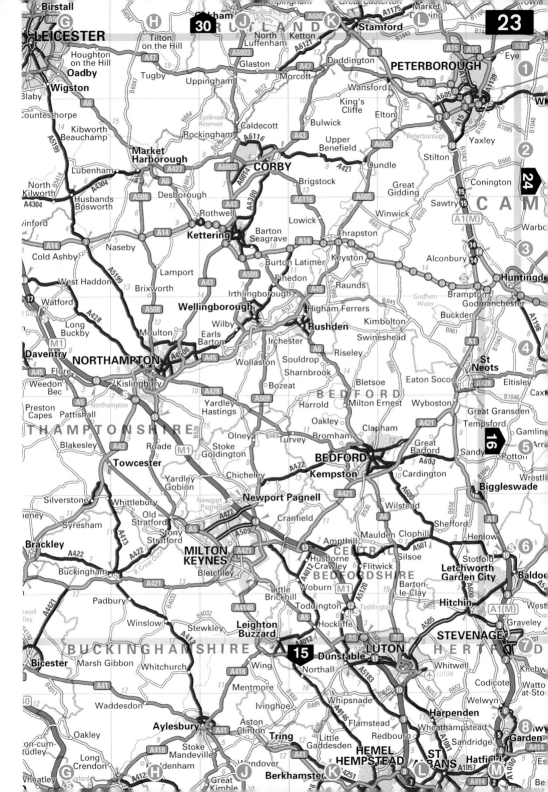

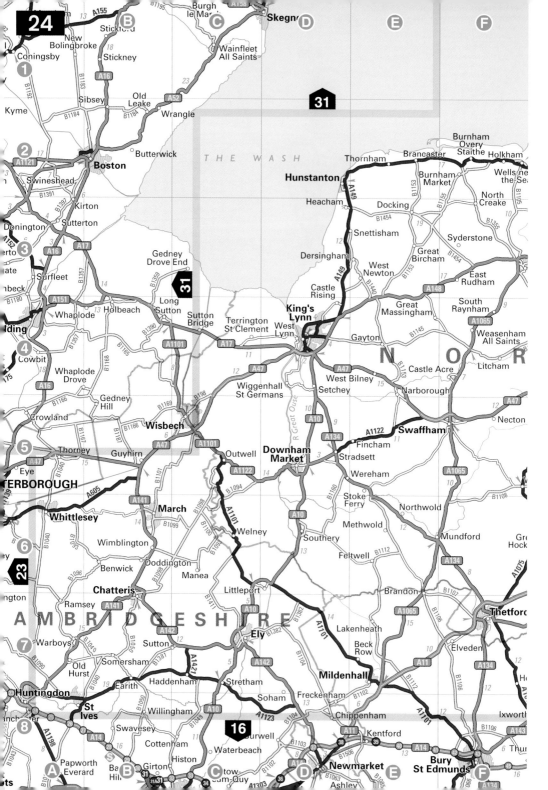

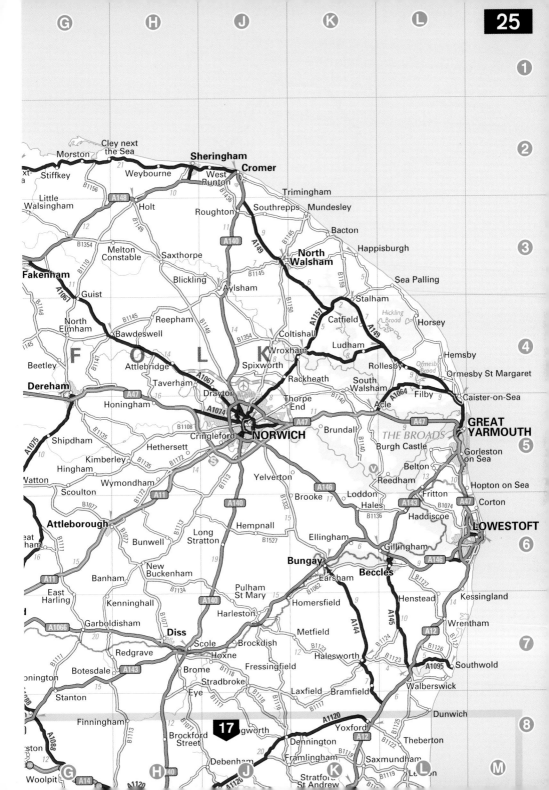

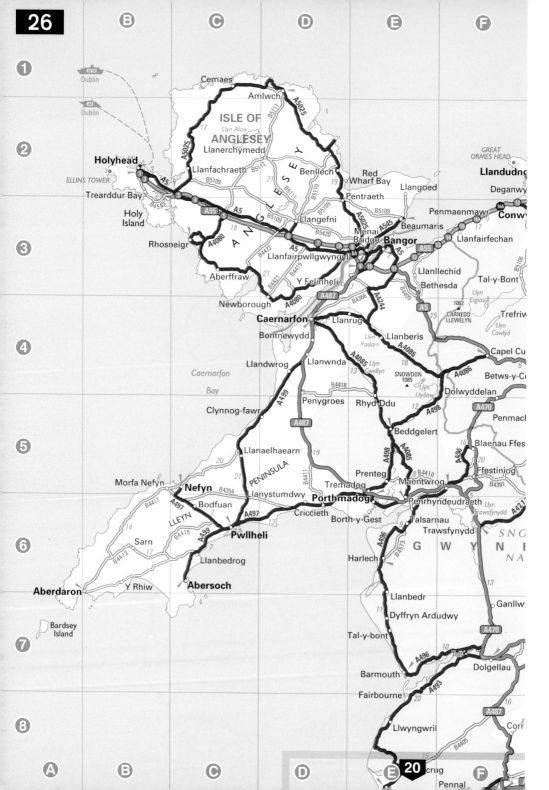

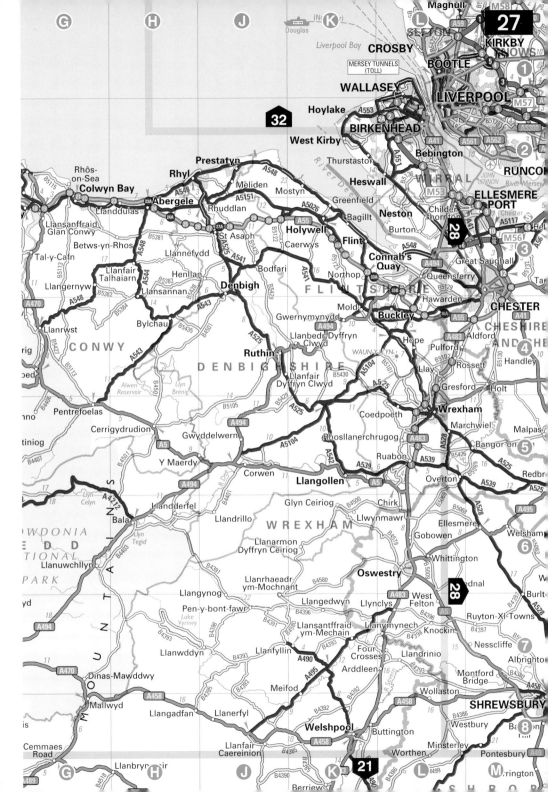

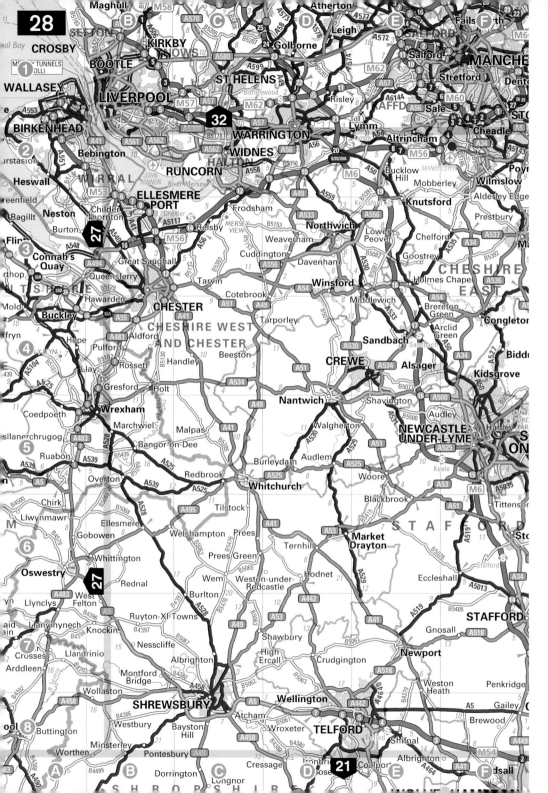

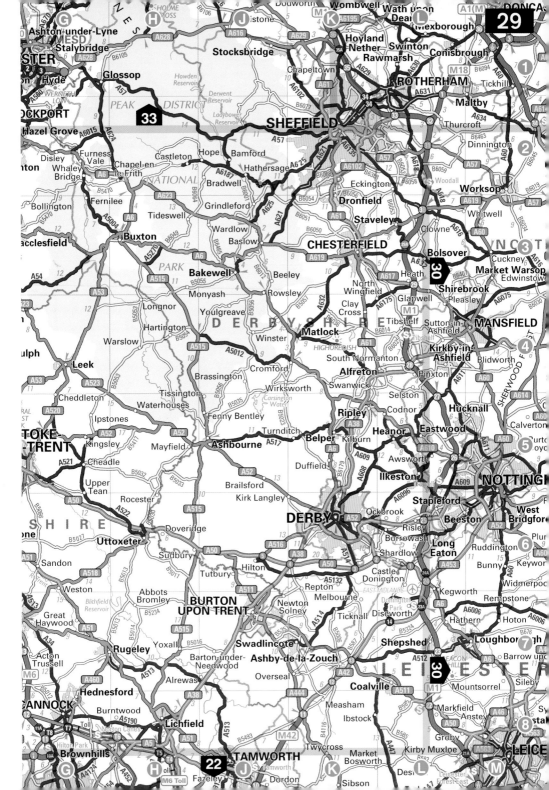

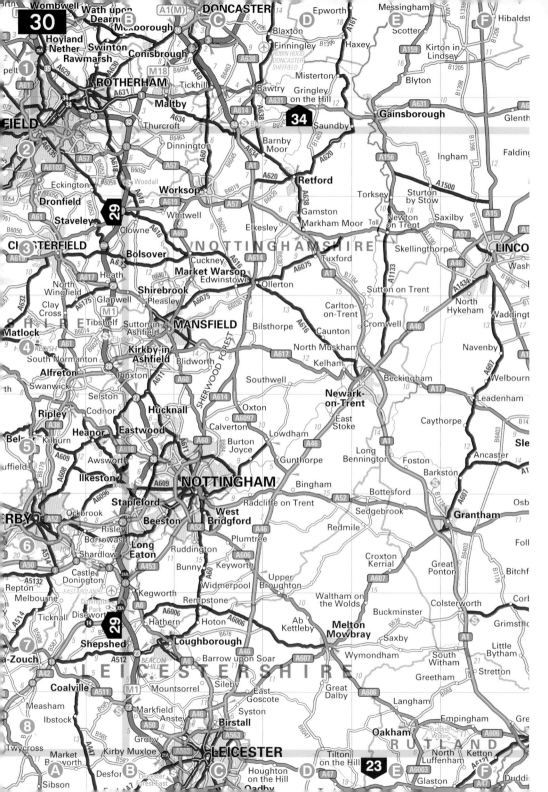

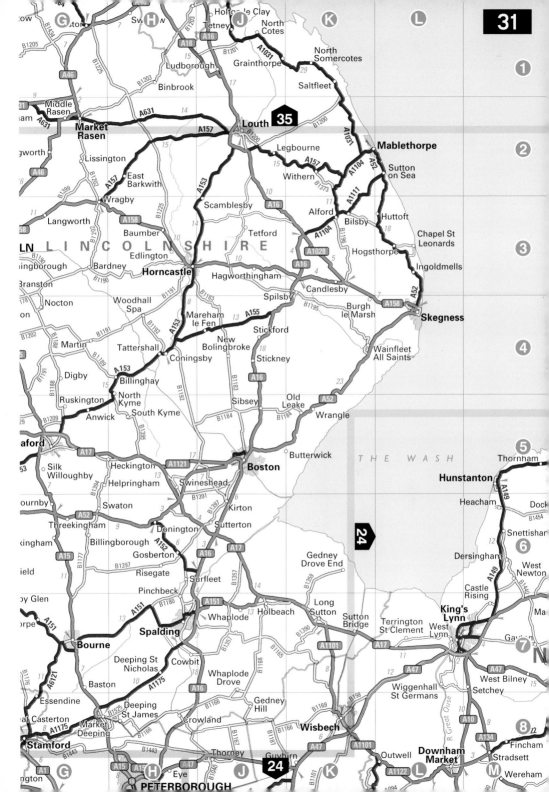

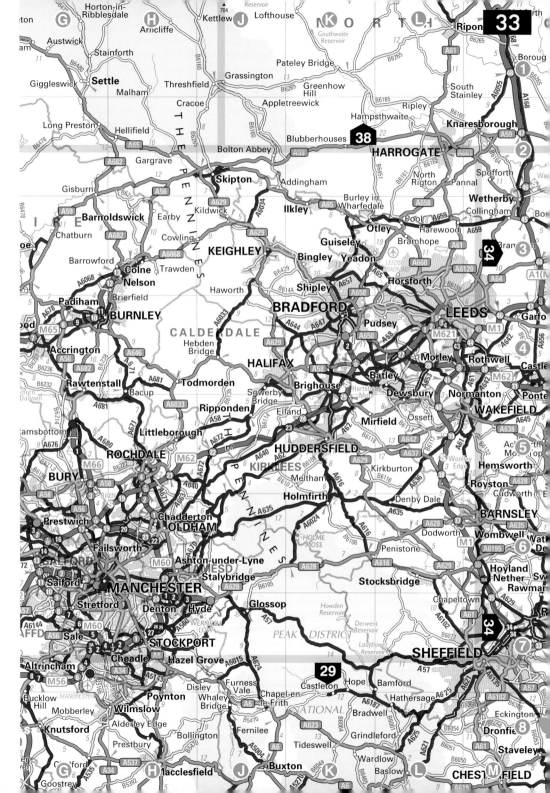

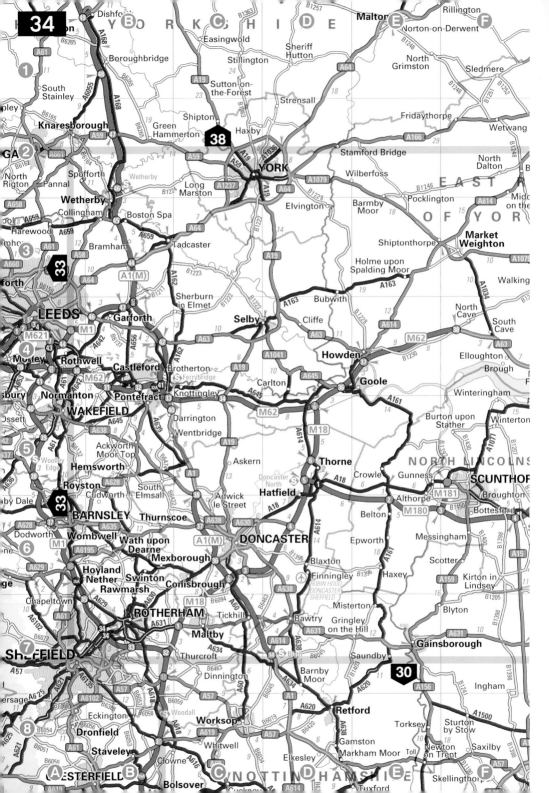

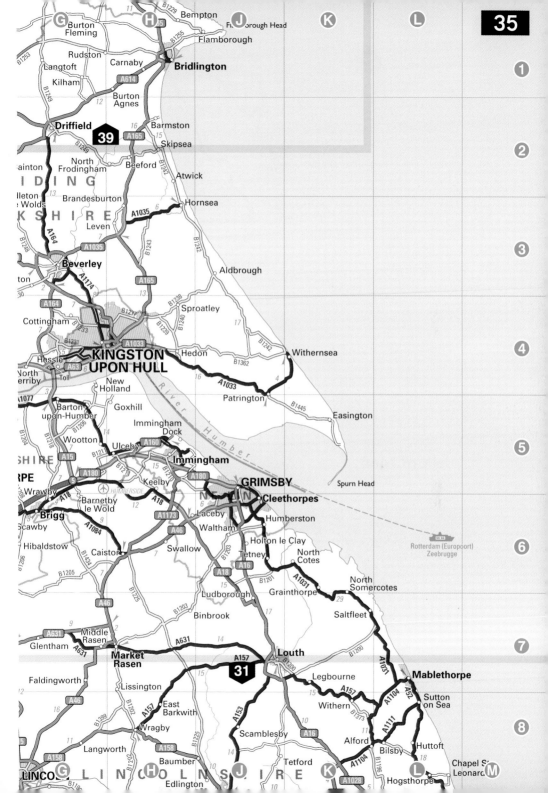

G H J K L

1
2
3
4
5
6
7
8

Bempton
Flamborough Head
Flamborough
**Bridlington**

Burton
Fleming
Rudston
Langtoft
Carnaby
Kilham
Burton
Agnes

**Driffield**
**39**
A614
A165
Barmston
Skipsea

ainton
North
Frodingham
Beeford
Atwick

IDING
Wolds
Brandesburton
Hornsea

KSHIRE
A1035
Leven

A164
A1035

**Beverley**
A165
Aldbrough

A1174
A164
Sproatley

Cottingham
B1238
B1239
B1240
17

B1231
B1297
**KINGSTON**
A1033
Hedon
Withernsea
B1362

Hessle
**UPON HULL**
Toll
New
Holland
B1242
4

North
erriby
A63
A1033
Patrington
B1445

A1077
Barton-
upon-Humber
Goxhill
Easington

B1204
B1218
Wootton
Immingham
Dock
River Humber

SHIRE
A15
Ulceby
A160

RPE
A180
Keelby
**GRIMSBY**
Spurn Head

Wrawby
A18
Barnetby
le Wold
A180
N
**Cleethorpes**

**Brigg**
A1173
Laceby
Humberston
Rotterdam (Europoort)
Zeebrugge

Scawby
A1084
A46
Waltham

Hibaldstow
Swallow
Holton le Clay
North
Cotes

B1205
B1434
Caistor
A16
Tetney
North
Somercotes

A46
B1225
A18
A1031
North

Middle
Rasen
Ludborough
Grainthorpe
29
Saltfleet

A631
A631
Binbrook
17

Glentham
A631
**Market
Rasen**
A631
A157
14
**Louth**
B1200
A1031
**Mablethorpe**

Faldingworth
A46
Lissington
**31**
Legbourne
A157
Sutton
on Sea

A157
East
Barkwith
A153
Withern
A1104
A52
A111

Langworth
A158
Wragby
B1225
Scamblesby
A16
10
Alford
Bilsby
Huttoft

A158
Baumber
Tetford
A1104
B1196
Chapel St
Leonards
M

LINCO
G
LN
H
OLMSJ
IRE
K
Edlington
A1028
Hogsthorpe
L

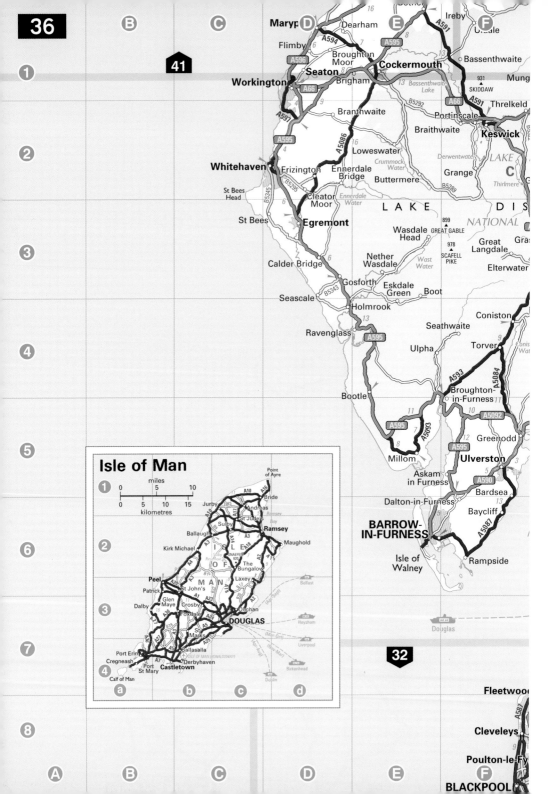

**B**     **C**     **D**     **E**     **F**

16

Ireby

Uldale

41

Dearham

Maryp **D**

A591

A594

7

Flimby

6

A596

Broughton
Moor

Cockermouth

Bassenthwaite

A595

8

Seaton

Brigham

A596

13

Bassenthwaite
Lake

931

SKIDDAW

Munq

**Workington**

A66

13

A591

A66

Threlkeld

4

A597

9

Branthwaite

Portinscale

A66

A591

A595

Braithwaite

**Keswick**

A5086

16

Loweswater

Crummock
Water

Derwentwater

LAKE

C

4

**Whitehaven**

Frizington

Ennerdale
Bridge

Buttermere

Grange

Thirlmere

DIS

St Bees
Head

B5295

Cleator
Moor

Ennerdale
Water

L A K E

NATIONAL

6

St Bees

**Egremont**

899
GREAT GABLE

978
SCAFELL
PIKE

Great
Langdale

Gra

B5345

Wasdale
Head

Calder Bridge

Nether
Wasdale

Wast
Water

Boot

Elterwater

Gosforth

Eskdale
Green

Seascale

Seathwaite

Coniston

Ravenglass

A595

13

Holmrook

A593

A5084

Conis
Wat

Ulpha

Torver

Bootle

Broughton-
in-Furness

11

A595

A5093

10

A5092

Greenodd

A595

12

8

Millom

A595

**Ulverston**

A590

5

Askam
in Furness

Bardsea

13

Dalton-in-Furness

Baycliff

**BARROW-
IN-FURNESS**

A5087

Isle of
Walney

Rampside

32

miles
0   5   10

0   5   10   15
kilometres

Point
of Ayre

A10

Jurby

Bride

Andreas

A9

Ramsey
Bay

Sulby

St Jude's

Ballaugh

**Ramsey**

Kirk Michael

I
L
E

Maughold

A14

A18

A15

The
Bungalow

**Peel**

M
A
N

Laxey

O
F

Patrick

St John's

A1

A22

Glen
Maye

Crosby

Onchan

Dalby

Foxdale

A5

**DOUGLAS**

St
Marks

Ballasalla

ISLE OF MAN RONALDSWAYS

Port Erin

A7

Cregneash

Port
St Mary

**Castletown**

Derbyhaven

Calf of Man

Belfast

Heysham

Liverpool

Douglas

Birkenhead

Dublin

**a**    **b**    **c**    **d**

Fleetwoo

A597

Cleveleys

Poulton-le-Fy

**BLACKPOOL**

**A**    **B**    **C**    **D**    **E**    **F**

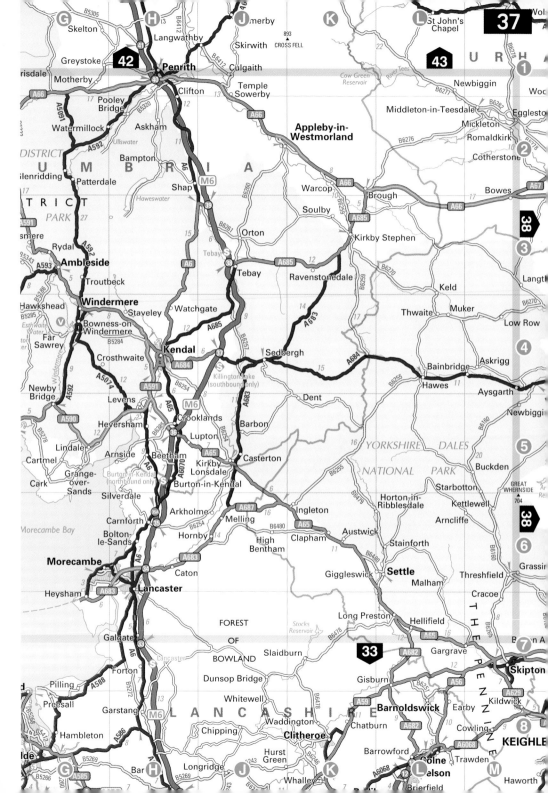

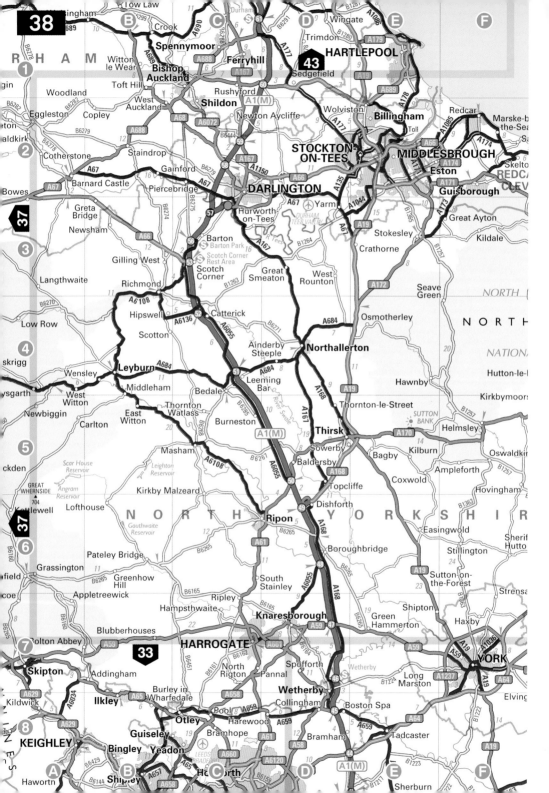

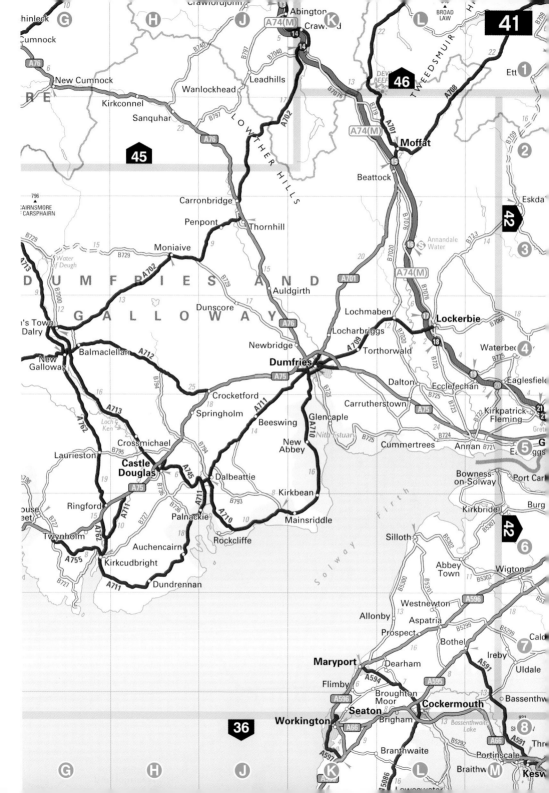

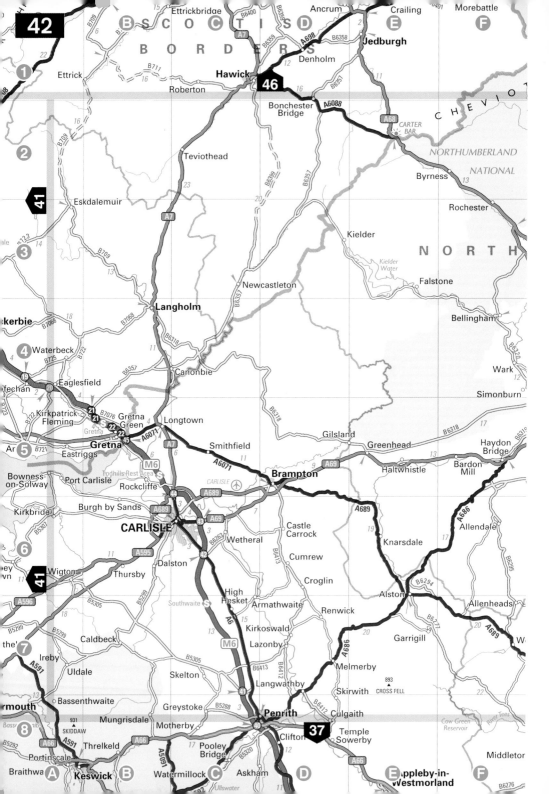

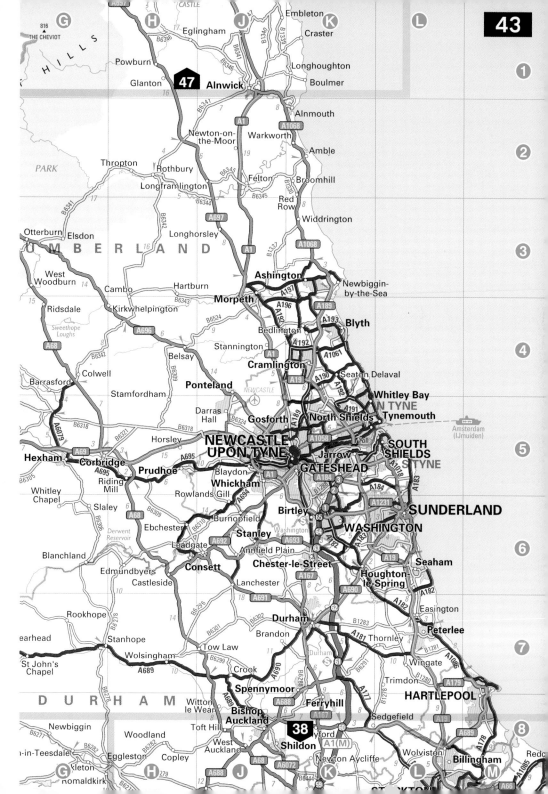

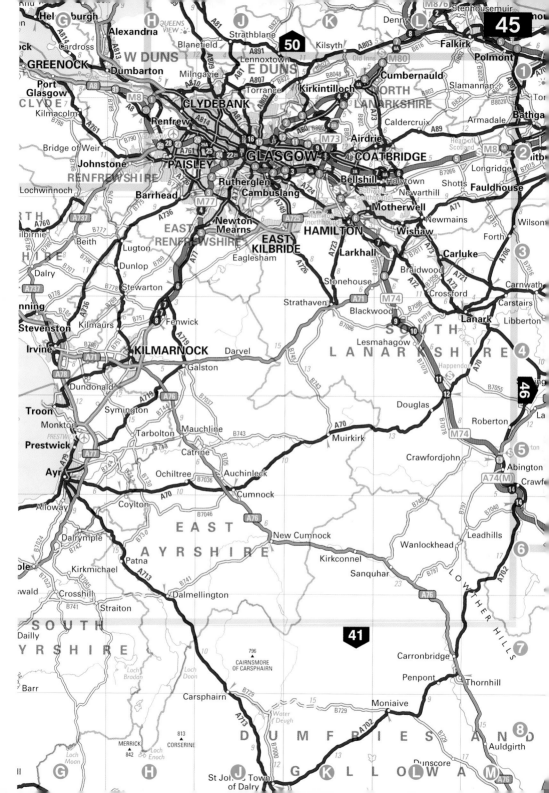

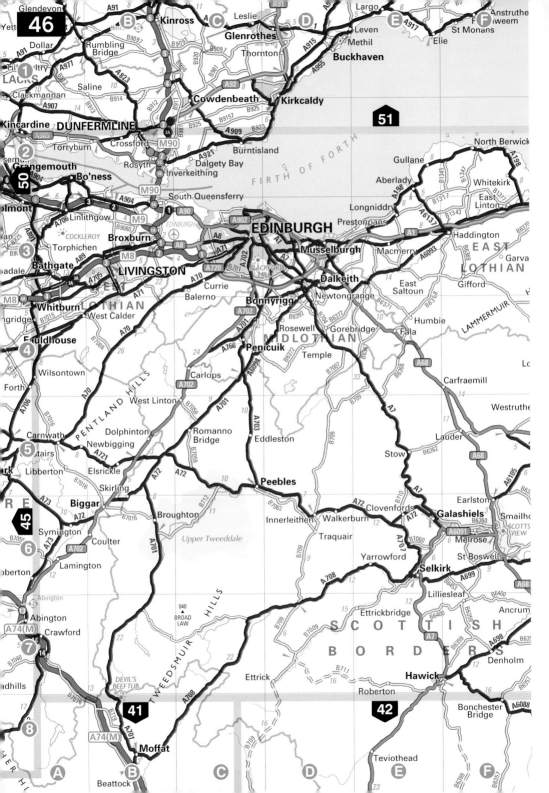

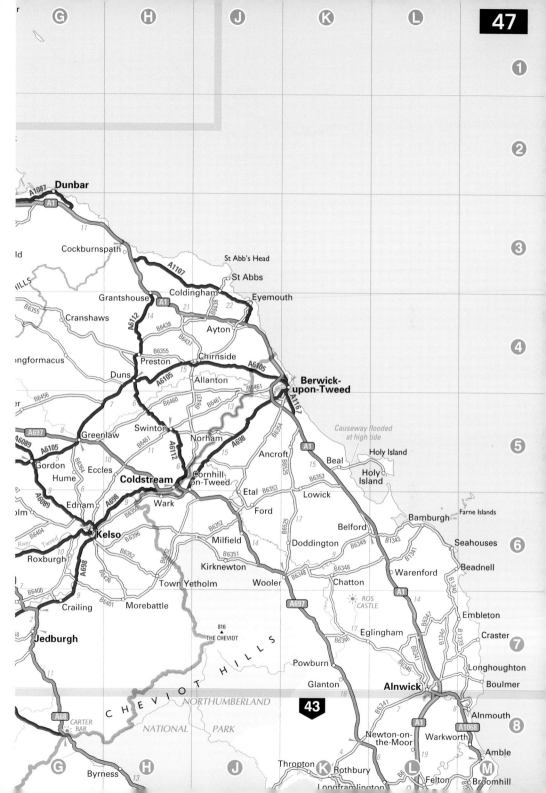

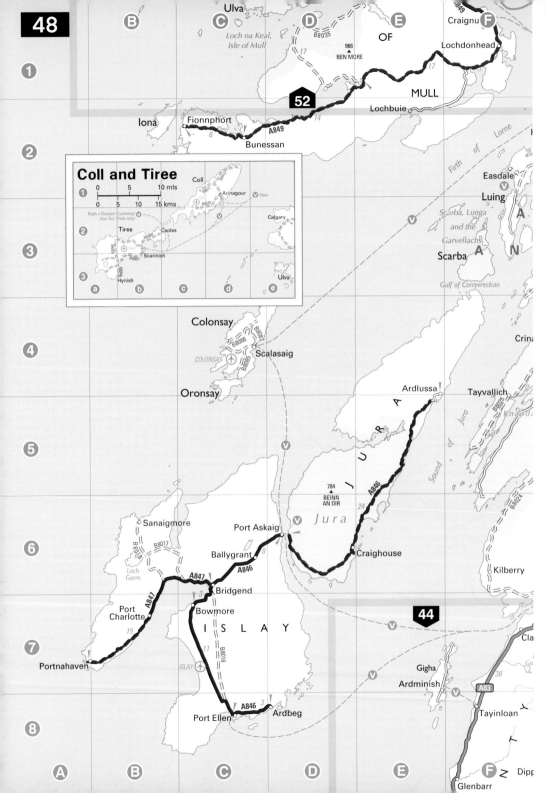

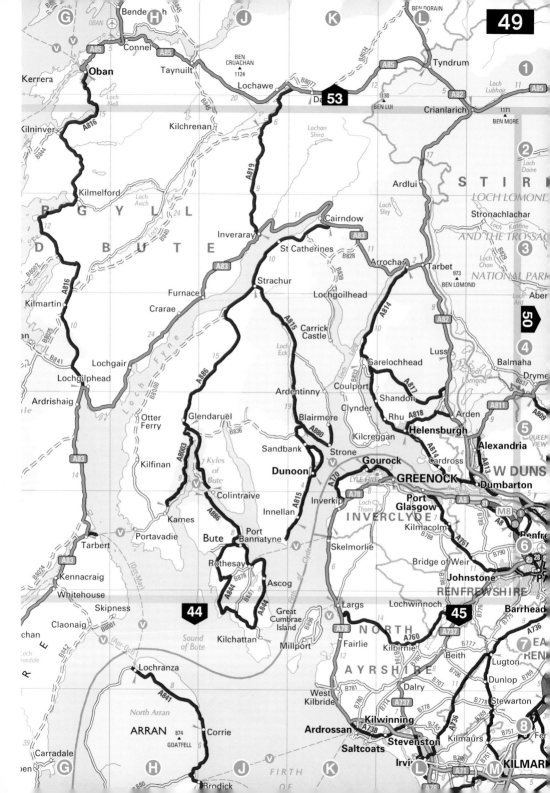

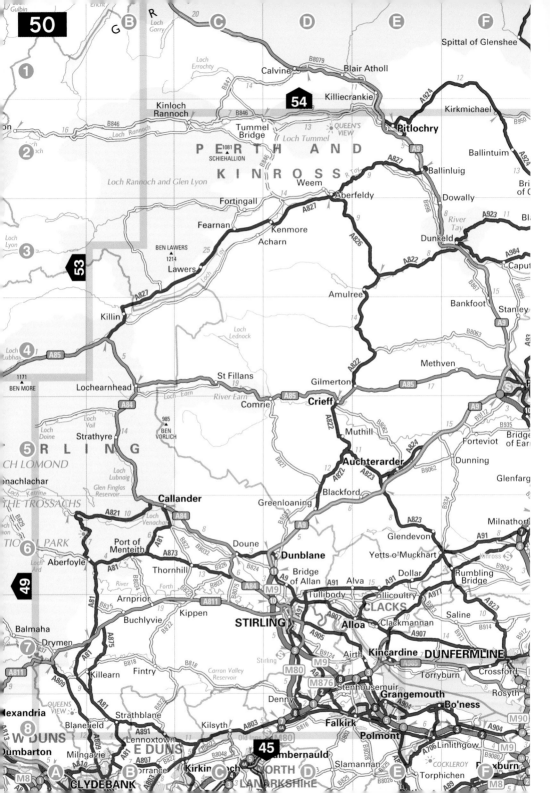

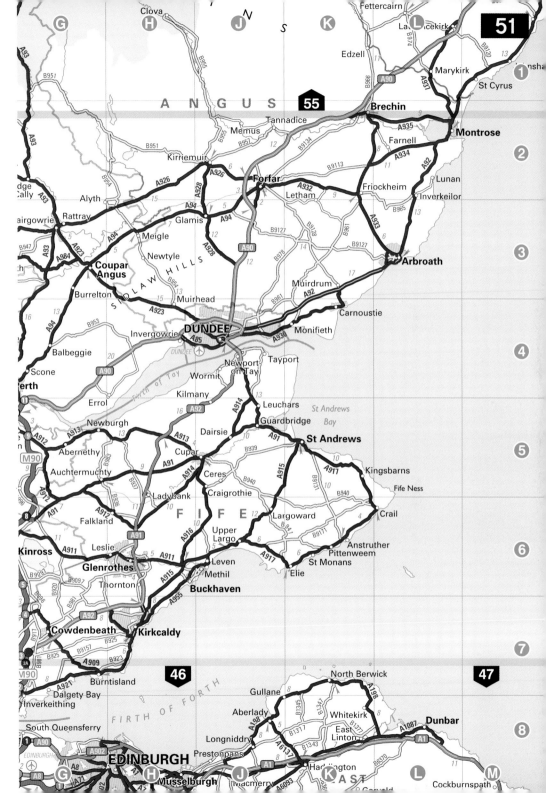

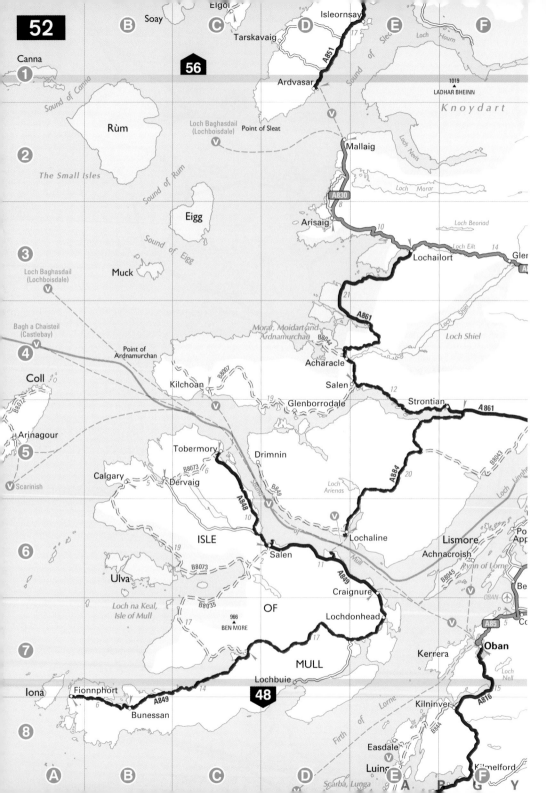

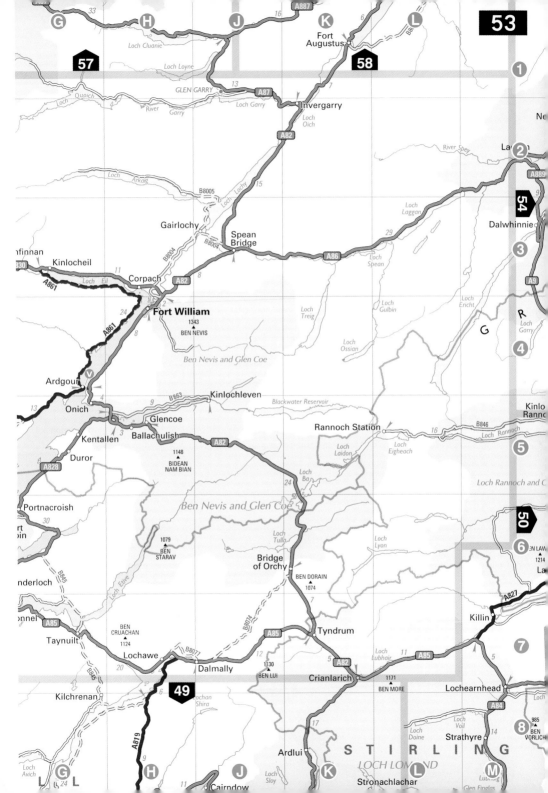

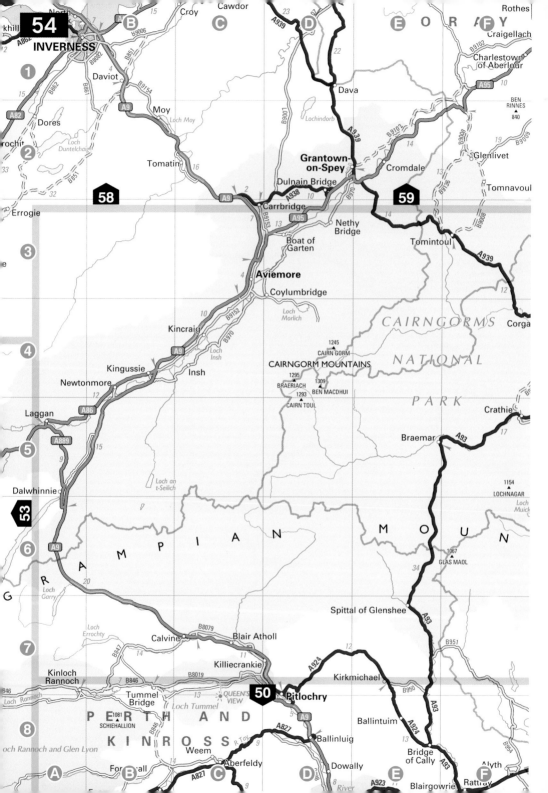

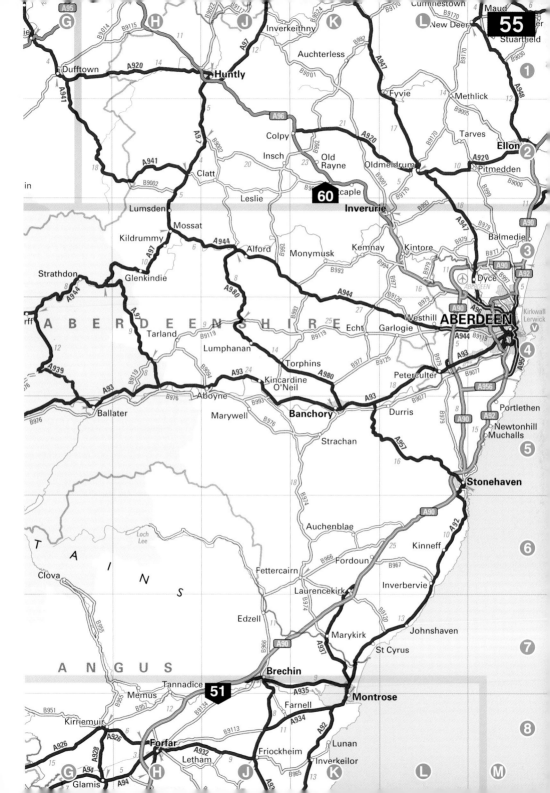

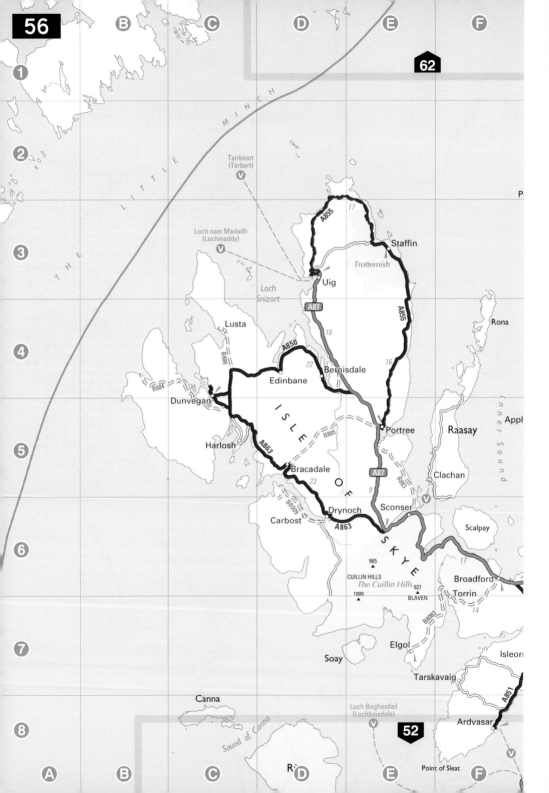

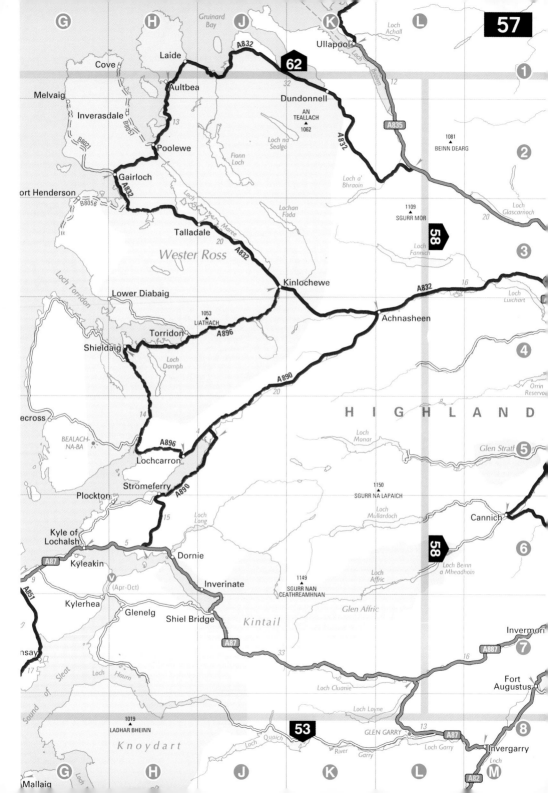

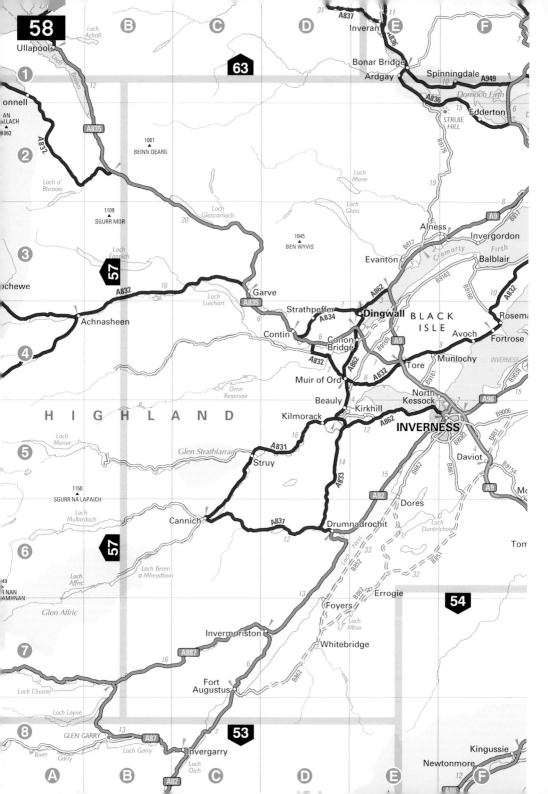

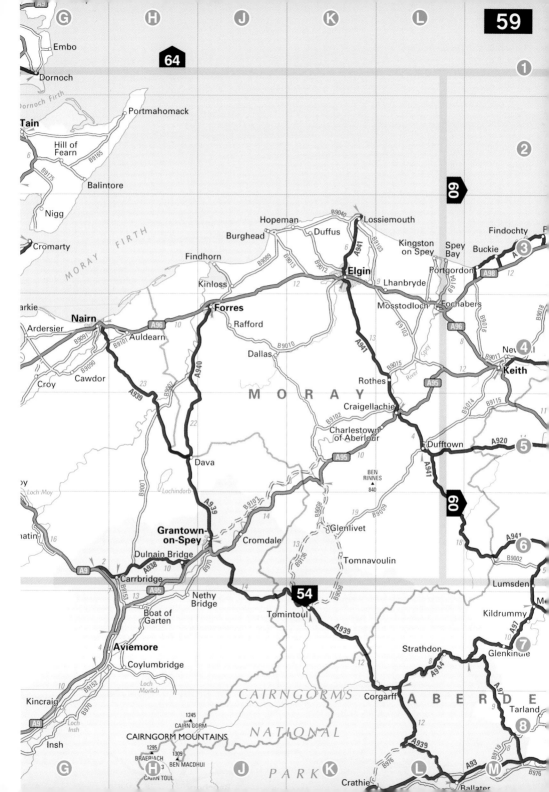

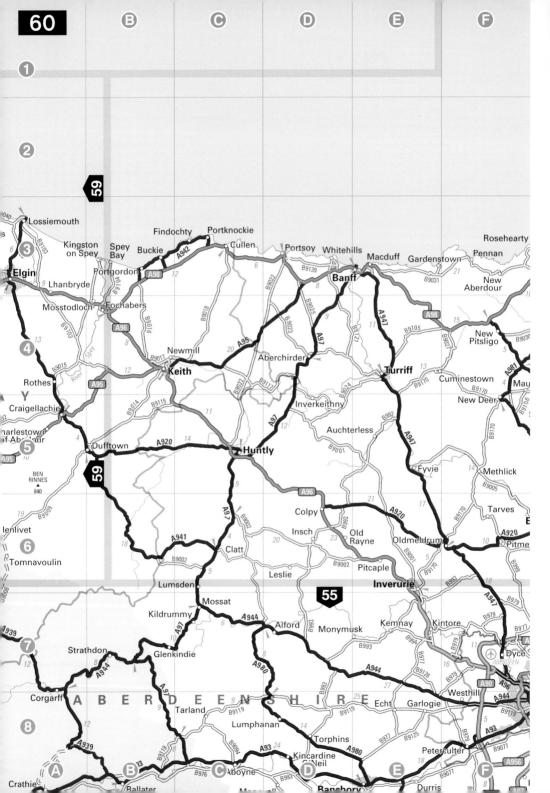

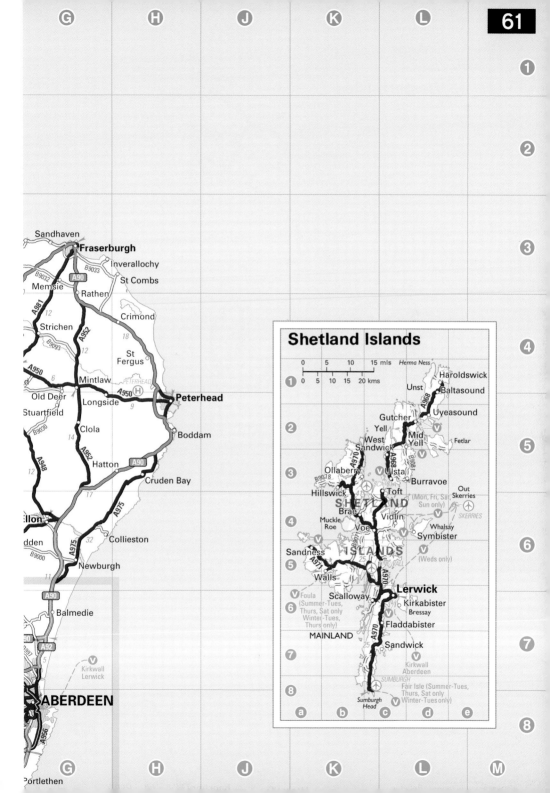

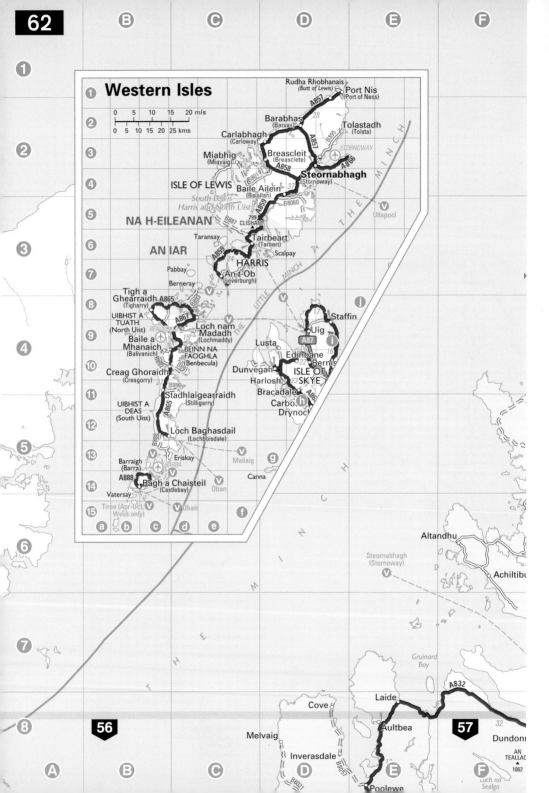

# Western Isles

0   5   10   15   20 mls

0  5  10 15 20 25 kms

Rudha Rhobhanais
(Butt of Lewis)

Port Nis
(Port of Ness)

A857

Barabhas
(Barvas)

28

Tolastadh
(Tolsta)

Carlabhagh
(Carloway)

B895

A857

STORNOWAY

Breascleit
(Breasclete)

A858

A866

Miabhig
(Miavaig)

**Steornabhagh**
(Stornoway)

ISLE OF LEWIS

B8011

Baile Ailein
(Balallan)

A859

B8060

South Lewis

NA H-EILEANAN

Harris and North Uist

A887

37

799
CLISHAM

Taransay

AN IAR

Tairbeart
(Tarbert)

24

Scalpay

Pabbay

A859

HARRIS

Berneray

An t-Ob
(Leverburgh)

V

THE LITTLE MINCH

Tigh a
Ghearraidh A865
(Tigharry)

B893

V

J

17

Staffin

UIBHIST A
TUATH
(North Uist)

A867

V

Uig

A87

16

BENBECULA

Loch nam
Madadh
(Lochmaddy)

Lusta

Edinbane

Bernis

Baile a
Mhanaich
(Balivanich)

15

BEINN NA
FAOGHLA
(Benbecula)

Dunvegan

22

ISLE OF
SKYE

Creag Ghoraidh
(Creagorry)

Harlosh

23

B890

Bracadale

A865

Stadhlaigearraidh
(Stilligarry)

Carbo

Drynoch

h

UIBHIST A
DEAS
(South Uist)

B888

Loch Baghasdail
(Lochboisdale)

V

Mallaig

g

Barraigh
(Barra)

V

Eriskay

Canna

A888

V

Bagh a Chaisteil
(Castlebay)

V

Oban

Vatersay

Tiree (Apr-Oct,
Weds only)

V

V

Oban

f

a   b   c   d   e

THE MINCH

H

Altandhu

Steornabhagh
(Stornoway)

V

Achiltibu

Gruinard
Bay

A832

Laide

Cove

Achiltibu

Melvaig

Aultbea

32

Dundoni

Inverasdale

B8021

B8057

AN
TEALLAC

1062

Loch na
Sealga

Poolewe

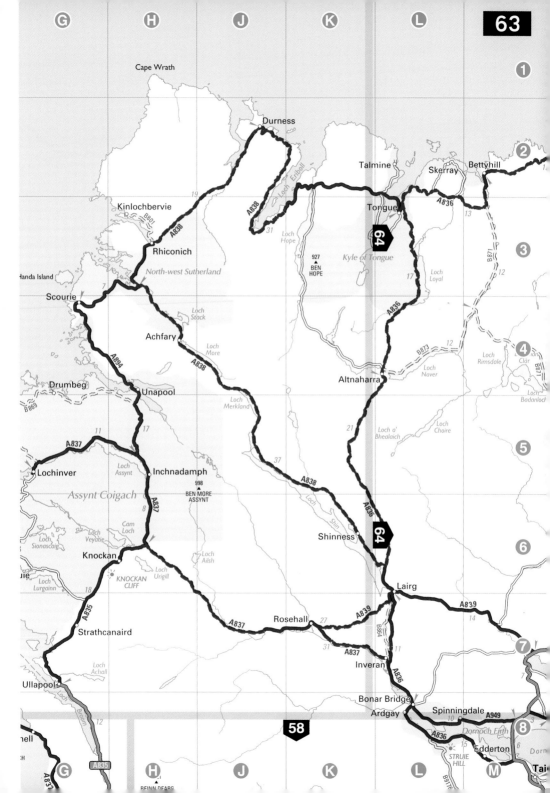

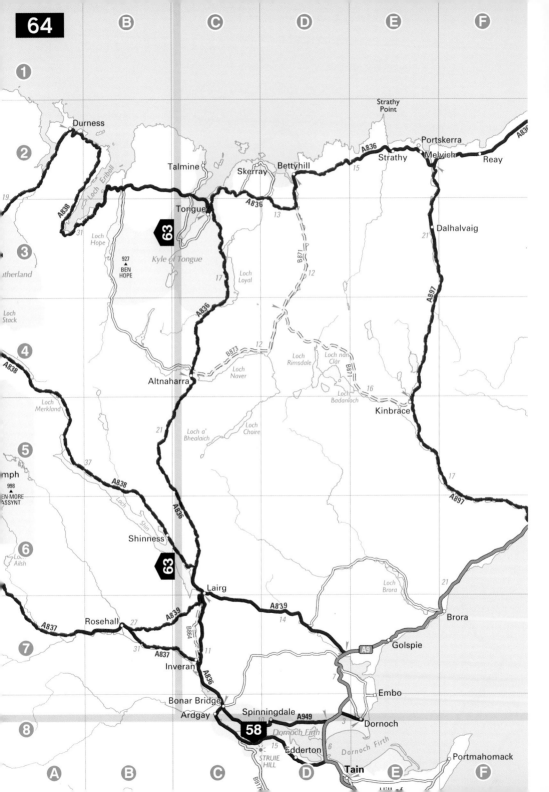

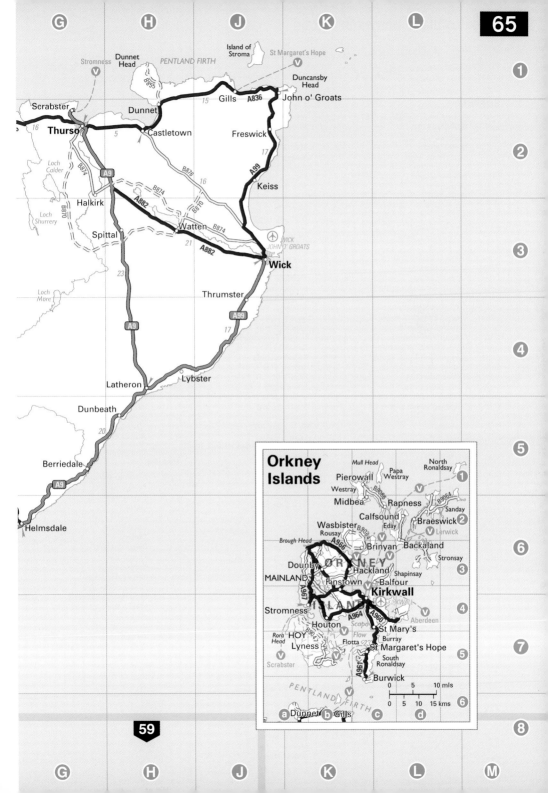

This index lists places appearing in the main-map section of the atlas in alphabetical order. The reference following each name gives the atlas page number and grid reference of the square in which the place appears. The map shows counties, unitary authorities and administrative areas, together with a list of the abbreviated name forms used in the index.

## England

| | |
|---|---|
| BaNES | **Bath & N E Somerset (18)** |
| Barns | **Barnsley (19)** |
| Bed | **Bedford** |
| Birm | **Birmingham** |
| Bl w D | **Blackburn with Darwen (20)** |
| Bmouth | **Bournemouth** |
| Bolton | **Bolton (21)** |
| Bpool | **Blackpool** |
| Br & H | **Brighton & Hove (22)** |
| Br For | **Bracknell Forest (23)** |
| Bristl | **City of Bristol** |
| Bucks | **Buckinghamshire** |
| Bury | **Bury (24)** |
| C Beds | **Central Bedfordshire** |
| C Brad | **City of Bradford** |
| C Derb | **City of Derby** |
| C KuH | **City of Kingston upon Hull** |
| C Leic | **City of Leicester** |
| C Nott | **City of Nottingham** |
| C Pete | **City of Peterborough** |
| C Plym | **City of Plymouth** |
| C Port | **City of Portsmouth** |
| C Sotn | **City of Southampton** |
| C Stke | **City of Stoke-on-Trent** |
| C York | **City of York** |
| Calder | **Calderdale (25)** |
| Cambs | **Cambridgeshire** |
| Ches E | **Cheshire East** |
| Ches W | **Cheshire West and Chester** |
| Cnwll | **Cornwall** |
| Covtry | **Coventry** |
| Cumb | **Cumbria** |
| Darltn | **Darlington (26)** |
| Derbys | **Derbyshire** |
| Devon | **Devon** |
| Donc | **Doncaster (27)** |
| Dorset | **Dorset** |
| Dudley | **Dudley (28)** |
| Dur | **Durham** |
| E R Yk | **East Riding of Yorkshire** |
| E Susx | **East Sussex** |
| Essex | **Essex** |
| Gatesd | **Gateshead (29)** |
| Gloucs | **Gloucestershire** |
| Gt Lon | **Greater London** |
| Halton | **Halton (30)** |
| Hants | **Hampshire** |
| Hartpl | **Hartlepool (31)** |
| Herefs | **Herefordshire** |
| Herts | **Hertfordshire** |
| IoS | **Isles of Scilly** |
| IoW | **Isle of Wight** |
| Kent | **Kent** |
| Kirk | **Kirklees (32)** |
| Knows | **Knowsley (33)** |
| Lancs | **Lancashire** |
| Leeds | **Leeds** |
| Leics | **Leicestershire** |
| Lincs | **Lincolnshire** |
| Lpool | **Liverpool** |
| Luton | **Luton** |
| M Keyn | **Milton Keynes** |
| Manch | **Manchester** |

| | |
|---|---|
| Medway | **Medway** |
| Middsb | **Middlesbrough** |
| N Linc | **North Lincolnshire** |
| N Som | **North Somerset (34)** |
| N Tyne | **North Tyneside (35)** |
| N u Ty | **Newcastle upon Tyne** |
| N York | **North Yorkshire** |
| NE Lin | **North East Lincolnshire** |
| Nhants | **Northamptonshire** |
| Norfk | **Norfolk** |
| Notts | **Nottinghamshire** |
| Nthumb | **Northumberland** |
| Oldham | **Oldham (36)** |
| Oxon | **Oxfordshire** |
| Poole | **Poole** |
| R & Cl | **Redcar & Cleveland** |
| Readg | **Reading** |
| Rochdl | **Rochdale (37)** |
| Rothm | **Rotherham (38)** |
| Rutlnd | **Rutland** |
| S Glos | **South Gloucestershire (39)** |
| S on T | **Stockton-on-Tees (40)** |
| S Tyne | **South Tyneside (41)** |
| Salfd | **Salford (42)** |
| Sandw | **Sandwell (43)** |
| Sefton | **Sefton (44)** |
| Sheff | **Sheffield** |
| Shrops | **Shropshire** |
| Slough | **Slough (45)** |
| Solhll | **Solihull (46)** |
| Somset | **Somerset** |
| St Hel | **St Helens (47)** |
| Staffs | **Staffordshire** |
| Sthend | **Southend-on-Sea** |
| Stockp | **Stockport (48)** |
| Suffk | **Suffolk** |
| Sundld | **Sunderland** |
| Surrey | **Surrey** |
| Swindn | **Swindon** |
| Tamesd | **Tameside (49)** |
| Thurr | **Thurrock (50)** |
| Torbay | **Torbay** |
| Traffd | **Trafford (51)** |
| W & M | **Windsor and Maidenhead (52)** |
| W Berk | **West Berkshire** |
| W Susx | **West Sussex** |
| Wakefd | **Wakefield (53)** |
| Warrtn | **Warrington (54)** |
| Warwks | **Warwickshire** |
| Wigan | **Wigan (55)** |
| Wilts | **Wiltshire** |
| Wirral | **Wirral (56)** |
| Wokham | **Wokingham (57)** |
| Wolves | **Wolverhampton (58)** |
| Worcs | **Worcestershire** |
| Wrekin | **Telford & Wrekin (59)** |
| Wsall | **Walsall (60)** |

## Channel Islands & Isle of Man

| | |
|---|---|
| Guern | **Guernsey** |
| Jersey | **Jersey** |
| IoM | **Isle of Man** |

## Scotland

| | |
|---|---|
| Abers | **Aberdeenshire** |
| Ag & B | **Argyll and Bute** |
| Angus | **Angus** |
| Border | **Scottish Borders** |
| C Aber | **City of Aberdeen** |
| C Dund | **City of Dundee** |
| C Edin | **City of Edinburgh** |
| C Glas | **City of Glasgow** |
| Clacks | **Clackmannanshire (1)** |
| D & G | **Dumfries & Galloway** |
| E Ayrs | **East Ayrshire** |
| E Duns | **East Dunbartonshire (2)** |
| E Loth | **East Lothian** |
| E Rens | **East Renfrewshire (3)** |
| Falk | **Falkirk** |
| Fife | **Fife** |
| Highld | **Highland** |
| Inver | **Inverclyde (4)** |
| Mdloth | **Midlothian (5)** |
| Moray | **Moray** |
| N Ayrs | **North Ayrshire** |
| N Lans | **North Lanarkshire (6)** |
| Ork | **Orkney Islands** |
| P & K | **Perth & Kinross** |
| Rens | **Renfrewshire (7)** |
| S Ayrs | **South Ayrshire** |
| S Lans | **South Lanarkshire (8)** |
| Shet | **Shetland Islands** |
| Stirlg | **Stirling** |
| W Duns | **West Dunbartonshire (8)** |
| W Isls | **Western Isles (Na h-Eileanan an Iar)** |
| W Loth | **West Lothian** |

## Wales

| | |
|---|---|
| Blae G | **Blaenau Gwent (9)** |
| Brdgnd | **Bridgend (10)** |
| Caerph | **Caerphilly (11)** |
| Cardif | **Cardiff** |
| Carmth | **Carmarthenshire** |
| Cerdgn | **Ceredigion** |
| Conwy | **Conwy** |
| Denbgs | **Denbighshire** |
| Flints | **Flintshire** |
| Gwynd | **Gwynedd** |
| IoA | **Isle of Anglesey** |
| Mons | **Monmouthshire** |
| Myr Td | **Merthyr Tydfil (12)** |
| Neath | **Neath Port Talbot (13)** |
| Newpt | **Newport (14)** |
| Pembks | **Pembrokeshire** |
| Powys | **Powys** |
| Rhondd | **Rhondda Cynon Taff (15)** |
| Swans | **Swansea** |
| Torfn | **Torfaen (16)** |
| V Glam | **Vale of Glamorgan (17)** |
| Wrexhm | **Wrexham** |

ORKNEY
ISLANDS

SHETLAND
ISLANDS

WESTERN ISLES (Na h-Eileanan an Iar)

HIGHLAND

MORAY

S C O T L A N D

ABERDEENSHIRE
Aberdeen

ANGUS

PERTH &
KINROSS
Dundee

ARGYLL
AND BUTE

STIRLING

FIFE

1
8  2
FALK  Edinburgh
4 Glasgow  W   E LOTH
7     6  LOTH
3        5
NORTH
AYRSHIRE

S LANS

SCOTTISH
BORDERS

E AYRS

S AYRS

DUMFRIES &
GALLOWAY

NORTHUMBERLAND
Newcastle
upon Tyne  35
29  41
Sunderland

CUMBRIA

DURHAM
31  R & CL
26  40  Middlesbrough

IoM

NORTH YORKSHIRE

Blackpool

LANCASHIRE
Bradford  York  EAST RIDING
OF YORKSHIRE
Leeds  Kingston
upon Hull
20  25
21 24 37  32  53  KE
55  36  19  N LINC  NE
44  33  42 49  27  LIN
47  51 Manchester  38
56  30 54 48 Sheffield
Liverpool
IoA
CONWY  FLINTS  CHES
W  CHES  DERBYS  NOTTS  LINCOLNSHIRE
DENBGS  E
Stoke-on-  Nottingham
GWYNEDD  WREXHAM  Trent  Derby
STAFFS
59  LEICS  RUTLAND  NORFOLK
SHROPSHIRE  58 60  Leicester  Peterborough
POWYS  28 43 Birmingham  CAMBS
46  Coventry
NHANTS  SUFFOLK
Milton  BED
WORCS  Keynes
CERDGN  HEREFS  WARWKS  BEDS Luton
W A L E S  E N G L A N D  HERTS  ESSEX
PEMBKS  9  MONS  GLOUCS  OXON  BUCKS  Southend-
CARMTH  12  16  Reading  52 45  GREATER  on-Sea
13  15 11  Swindon  W BERK  57 23  LONDON  50
Swansea 10  14  39  SURREY  MEDWAY
17  Cardiff  Bristol  WILTSHIRE
34  18  HAMPSHIRE  KENT
W SUSX  E SUSX
SOMERSET  22
Southampton
DEVON  DORSET  Portsmouth
Bournemouth  IoW
Poole
CORNWALL  GUERNSEY
Plymouth  Torbay  CHANNEL
ISLANDS  Jersey
IoS

## A

Abberley Worcs.............21 L4
Abbey Town Cumb......41 L6
Abbots Bromley
 Staffs..........................29 H7
Aberaeron Cerdgn......19 H1
Aberarth Cerdgn.........19 H1
Aberchirder Abers......60 D4
Aberdare Rhondd.........12 B2
Aberdaron Gwynd.......26 B6
Aberdeen C Aber.........55 M4
Aberdyfi Gwynd..........20 A2
Aberfeldy P & K...........50 D2
Aberffraw IoA..............26 C3
Aberfoyle Stirlg...........50 B6
Abergavenny Mons......21 G8
Abergele Conwy..........27 H3
Aberlady E Loth...........46 E2
Aberlour,
 Charlestown of
 Moray..........................59 L5
Abermule Powys..........20 F2
Abernethy P & K..........51 G5
Aberporth Cerdgn.......18 F2
Abersoch Gwynd.........26 C6
Abersychan Torfn........12 D2
Abertillery Blae G........12 D2
Aberystwyth Cerdgn...20 A3
Abingdon-on-
 Thames Oxon............14 C4
Abington S Lans..........45 M5
Ab Kettleby Leics.........30 D7
Aboyne Abers..............55 J4
Abridge Essex..............16 D7
Accrington Lancs.........33 G4
Acharacle Highld.........52 D4
Acharn P & K...............50 C3
Achfary Highld.............63 H4
Achiltibuie Highld........62 F6
Achnacroish Ag & B....52 F6
Achnasheen Highld.....57 L4
Ackworth Moor Top
 Wakefd........................34 B5
Acle Norfk....................25 K5
Acton Trussell Staffs...29 G2
Addingham C Brad......33 J2
Adwick le Street
 Donc...........................34 C6
Ainderby Steeple
 N York.........................38 D4
Airdrie N Lans..............45 L2
Airth Falk.....................50 E7
Albrighton Shrops.......21 L1
Albrighton Shrops.......28 C7
Albury Surrey................9 K2
Alcester Warwks..........22 B4
Alconbury Cambs........23 M3
Aldborough E R Yk.......35 J3
Aldbourne Wilts...........14 A6
Aldbrough E R Yk.........35 J3
Aldeburgh Suffk..........17 M2
Alderbury Wilts..............8 C3
Alderley Edge Ches E...28 F3
Aldermaston W Berk....14 D7
Alderminster Warwks...22 D5
Aldershot Hants............9 H2
Aldford Ches W............28 B4
Aldham Essex...............17 G5
Alexandria W Duns......49 M5
Alfold Surrey..................9 K3
Alford Abers.................55 J3
Alford Lincs..................31 K3
Alfreton Derbys............29 L4
Alfriston E Susx............10 D7
Alkham Kent................11 K4
Allanton Border...........47 H4
Allendale Nthumb........42 F6
Allenheads Nthumb......42 F7
Allensmore Herefs.......21 J6
Alloa Clacks.................50 E7
Allonby Cumb..............41 L7
Alloway S Ayrs.............45 G6
Almondsbury S Glos....13 G3
Alness Highld..............58 F3
Alnmouth Nthumb.......43 K2
Alnwick Nthumb..........47 J7
Alrewas Staffs.............29 J7
Alsager Ches E............28 E4
Alston Cumb.................42 E6
Altandhu Highld...........62 F6
Althorpe N Linc...........34 E5
Altnaharra Highld........64 C4
Alton Hants....................9 H2
Alton Pancras Dorset....7 K2
Altrincham Traffd.........28 E2
Alva Clacks..................50 E6
Alveston S Glos............13 G3
Alyth P & K..................51 G3
Amberley W Susx..........9 K4
Amble Nthumb.............43 K2

Ambleside Cumb..........37 G3
Amersham Bucks.........15 G4
Amesbury Wilts.............8 C2
Amlwch IoA..................26 D1
Ammanford Carmth......19 J5
Ampleforth N York........38 F5
Ampthill C Beds...........23 K6
Amroth Pembks...........18 E5
Amulree P & K.............50 E3
Ancaster Lincs.............30 F5
Ancroft Nthumb...........47 K5
Ancrum Border.............47 G7
Andover Hants...............8 D2
Andoversford Gloucs...22 B7
Andreas IoM.................36 c1
Angle Pembks..............18 C6
Angmering W Susx........9 K5
Annan D & G................41 M5
Annfield Plain Dur.......43 J6
Anstey Leics.................30 C8
Anstruther Fife............51 K6
An t-Ob W Isls.............62 e7
Anwick Lincs................31 G5
Appleby-in-
 Westmorland
 Cumb...........................37 J2
Applecross Highld.......57 G5
Appledore Devon..........4 D4
Appledore Kent............11 H5
Appletreewick
 N York.........................38 A7
Arbroath Angus...........51 L3
Arclid Green Ches E.....28 E4
Ardbeg Ag & B.............48 D8
Arddleen Powys............27 L7
Arden Ag & B................49 L5
Ardentinny Ag & B.......49 K4
Ardersier Highld...........59 G4
Ardgay Highld..............64 C8
Ardgour Highld.............53 G4
Ardingly W Susx...........10 C5
Ardleigh Essex.............17 H4
Ardlui Ag & B...............49 L2
Ardlussa Ag & B..........48 E4
Ardminish Ag & B........44 A3
Ardrishaig Ag & B........49 G5
Ardrossan N Ayrs.........44 F4
Ardvasar Highld...........52 D1
Ardwell D & G..............40 C7
Arinagour Ag & B.........48 d1
Arisaig Highld...............52 D3
Arkholme Lancs...........37 J6
Armadale W Loth.........45 M2
Armathwaite Cumb.......42 C7
Arncliffe N York............37 M6
Arnprior Stirlg..............50 B7
Arnside Cumb...............37 H5
Arrington Cambs..........16 B3
Arrochar Ag & B...........49 L3
Arundel W Susx.............9 K5
Ascog Ag & B...............49 J6
Ascot W & M................15 G6
Ash Kent......................11 K3
Ashbourne Derbys.......29 J5
Ashburton Devon...........6 B7
Ashbury Oxon..............14 A5
Ashby-de-la-Zouch
 Leics...........................29 K7
Ashcott Somset...........12 E7
Ashford Kent................11 H4
Ashington W Susx........43 K3
Ashington W Susx.........9 L4
Ashley Cambs..............16 E2
Ashton-under-Lyne
 Tamesd.......................33 H6
Ashurst Hants................8 D5
Ashwater Devon............4 D7
Askam in Furness
 Cumb...........................36 F5
Askern Donc.................34 C5
Askham Cumb..............37 H2
Askrigg N York.............37 M4
Aspatria Cumb.............41 L7
Aston Oxon...................14 B4
Aston Clinton Bucks....14 F3
Aston on Clun Shrops...21 H3
Aston Rowant Oxon......14 E4
Atcham Shrops............28 C8
Atherstone Warwks......22 D1
Atherton Wigan............32 F6
Attleborough Norfk......25 H4
Attlebridge Norfk.........25 H4
Atwick E R Yk...............35 H2
Auchenblae Abers........55 K6
Auchencairn D & G......41 H6
Auchinleck E Ayrs.........45 J5
Auchterarder P & K.......50 E5
Auchterless Abers........60 E5
Auchtermuchty Fife.....51 G5
Audlem Ches E.............28 D5
Audley Staffs................28 E5
Auldearn Highld...........59 H4

Auldgirth D & G...........41 J3
Aultbea Highld.............57 H1
Austwick N York...........37 K6
Avebury Wilts...............13 L4
Avening Gloucs............13 J2
Aveton Gifford
 Devon............................6 A6
Aviemore Highld..........54 C3
Avoch Highld................58 F4
Avonmouth Bristl.........12 F4
Awsworth Notts............30 B5
Axbridge Somset..........12 E5
Axminster Devon............6 F3
Axmouth Devon.............6 F3
Aylesbury Bucks..........14 F3
Aylesham Kent.............11 K3
Aylsham Norfk..............25 J3
Aynho Nhants..............22 F6
Ayr S Ayrs....................45 G5
Aysgarth N York...........38 A4
Ayton Border................47 J4

## B

Backaland Ork.............65 d2
Bacton Norfk................25 K3
Bacup Lancs................33 H4
Bagby N York...............38 E5
Bagh a Chaisteil
 W Isls........................62 b14
Bagillt Flints................27 K3
Baglan Neath...............19 K6
Bagshot Surrey............14 F7
Baile Ailein W Isls........62 g4
Baile a Mhanaich
 W Isls.......................62 c10
Bainbridge N York.......37 M4
Bainton E R Yk............34 F2
Bakewell Derbys..........29 J3
Bala Gwynd..................27 H6
Balallan W Isls.............62 g4
Balbeggie P & K...........51 G4
Balblair Highld..............58 F3
Balcombe W Susx........10 B5
Baldersby N York..........38 D5
Baldock Herts..............16 B4
Balerno C Edin.............46 C3
Balfour Ork..................65 c3
Balintore Highld...........59 G2
Balivanich W Isls.......62 c10
Ballachulish Highld......53 H5
Ballantrae S Ayrs.........40 B4
Ballasalla IoM..............36 b4
Ballater Abers..............55 G5
Ballaugh IoM................36 c2
Ballinluig P & K............50 E2
Ballintuim P & K...........50 F2
Ballygrant Ag & B........48 C6
Balmaclellan D & G......41 G4
Balmaha Stirlg.............49 M4
Balmedie Abers...........55 M3
Balsall Common Solhll...22 D3
Balsham Cambs............16 E3
Baltasound Shet..........61 d1
Bamber Bridge Lancs...32 E4
Bamburgh Nthumb.......47 L6
Bamford Derbys...........29 J2
Bampton Cumb............37 H2
Bampton Devon.............5 H5
Bampton Oxon.............14 A4
Banbury Oxon..............22 E6
Banchory Abers...........55 K5
Banff Abers..................60 E3
Bangor Gwynd.............26 E3
Bangor-on-Dee
 Wrexhm......................28 B5
Banham Norfk..............25 H6
Bankfoot P & K............50 F4
Banstead Surrey..........10 B3
Banwell N Som............12 E5
Barabhas W Isls...........62 h2
Barbon Cumb...............37 J5
Bardney Lincs..............31 G3
Bardon Mill Nthumb....42 F6
Bardsea Cumb.............36 F5
Barford Warwks...........22 D4
Bargoed Caerph..........12 C2
Bar Hill Cambs............16 C2
Barking Gt Lon............16 C8
Barkston Lincs.............30 F5
Barkway Herts..............16 C4
Barley Herts..................16 C4
Barmby Moor E R Yk....34 E2
Barmouth Gwynd.........26 F7
Barmston E R Yk...........39 L7
Barnard Castle Dur......38 A2
Barnby Moor Notts......30 D2
Barnet Gt Lon..............15 J4
Barnetby le Wold
 N Linc.........................35 G6

Barnoldswick Lancs....33 H3
Barnsley Barns............33 M6
Barnsley Gloucs..........13 L2
Barnstaple Devon..........4 E4
Barr S Ayrs...................40 D3
Barrasford Nthumb......43 G4
Barrhead E Rens..........45 H3
Barrhill S Ayrs..............40 D4
Barrowford Lancs.........33 H3
Barrow-in-Furness
 Cumb...........................36 E6
Barrow upon Soar
 Leics...........................30 C7
Barry V Glam................5 K1
Barton Cambs..............16 C2
Barton Lancs................32 E3
Barton N York..............38 C3
Barton-le-Clay
 C Beds.........................23 L7
Barton-on-Sea Hants....8 C6
Barton Seagrave
 Nhants.........................23 J3
Barton-under-
 Needwood Staffs......29 J7
Barton-upon-
 Humber N Linc..........35 G5
Barvas W Isls...............62 h2
Barwell Leics...............22 E2
Basildon Essex............16 F7
Basingstoke Hants........9 G1
Baslow Derbys.............29 J3
Bassenthwaite
 Cumb...........................42 A8
Baston Lincs.................31 G7
Bathgate W Loth..........46 A3
Batley Kirk...................33 L4
Battle E Susx................10 F6
Baumber Lincs.............31 H3
Bawdeswell Norfk.......25 H4
Bawdsey Suffk.............17 L4
Bawtry Donc................34 D7
Baycliff Cumb...............36 F6
Bayston Hill Shrops......28 C8
Beaconsfield Bucks.....15 G5
Beadnell Nthumb.........47 L6
Beaford Devon...............4 E5
Beal Nthumb................47 K5
Beaminster Dorset........7 H2
Beare Green Surrey........9 L2
Bearsted Kent..............10 F3
Beattock D & G............41 L2
Beaulieu Hants..............8 E5
Beauly Highld..............58 D5
Beaumaris IoA.............26 E3
Beaumont Jersey..........7 b2
Beaworthy Devon...........4 D7
Bebington Wirral..........27 L2
Beccles Suffk...............25 L6
Beckhampton Wilts......13 L4
Beckingham Lincs........30 E4
Beckington Somset......13 H6
Beck Row Suffk............24 E7
Bedale N York...............38 C4
Bedgellert Gwynd.........26 E5
Bedford Bed.................23 K5
Bedlington Nthumb......43 K4
Bedworth Warwks.........22 E2
Beeford E R Yk.............35 H2
Beeley Derbys..............29 J3
Beer Devon....................6 F3
Beesands Devon............6 B7
Beeston Ches W...........28 C4
Beeston Notts..............30 B6
Beeswing D & G...........41 J5
Beetham Cumb.............37 H5
Beetley Norfk...............25 G4
Beguildy Powys............20 F3
Beith N Ayrs.................45 G3
Belford Nthumb...........47 L6
Bellingham Nthumb......42 F4
Bellochantuy Ag & B....44 A5
Bellshill N Lans............45 K2
Belper Derbys...............29 K5
Belsay Nthumb.............43 H4
Belton N Linc...............34 E6
Belton Norfk.................25 L5
Bembridge IoW..............9 G6
Bempton E R Yk...........39 L6
Benderloch Ag & B......52 F6
Benenden Kent............10 F5
Benllech IoA.................26 D2
Benson Oxon...............14 D5
Bentley Hants................9 H2
Benwick Cambs...........24 B6
Bere Alston Devon.........3 K4
Bere Ferrers Devon........3 K4
Bere Regis Dorset.........7 L3
Berkeley Gloucs...........13 G2
Berkhamsted Herts......15 G3
Bernisdale Highld........56 D4
Berriedale Highld.........65 G5

| Place | County | Page | Grid |
|---|---|---|---|
| Berriew | Powys | 20 | F1 |
| Berrow | Somset | 12 | D6 |
| Berwick St John | Wilts | 13 | K8 |
| Berwick-upon-Tweed | Nthumb | 47 | K4 |
| Bethersden | Kent | 11 | G4 |
| Bethesda | Gwynd | 26 | E3 |
| Bettyhill | Highld | 64 | D2 |
| Betws-y-Coed | Conwy | 27 | G4 |
| Betws-yn-Rhos | Conwy | 27 | H3 |
| Beulah | Powys | 20 | D5 |
| Beverley | E R Yk | 35 | G3 |
| Bewdley | Worcs | 21 | L3 |
| Bexhill | E Susx | 10 | F7 |
| Bibury | Gloucs | 13 | L1 |
| Bicester | Oxon | 14 | D2 |
| Bickleigh | Devon | 5 | M6 |
| Biddenden | Kent | 11 | G4 |
| Biddisham | Somset | 12 | E6 |
| Biddulph | Staffs | 28 | F4 |
| Bideford | Devon | 4 | D5 |
| Bidford-on-Avon | Warwks | 22 | C5 |
| Bigbury-on-Sea | Devon | 3 | M6 |
| Biggar | S Lans | 46 | B6 |
| Biggin Hill | Gt Lon | 10 | C3 |
| Biggleswade | C Beds | 23 | M5 |
| Bildeston | Suffk | 17 | H3 |
| Billericay | Essex | 16 | E7 |
| Billingborough | Lincs | 31 | G6 |
| Billingham | S on T | 38 | E2 |
| Billinghay | Lincs | 31 | H4 |
| Billingshurst | W Susx | 9 | K3 |
| Bilsby | Lincs | 31 | K3 |
| Bilsthorpe | Notts | 30 | C4 |
| Binbrook | Lincs | 35 | H7 |
| Binfield | Br For | 14 | F6 |
| Bingham | Notts | 30 | D5 |
| Bingley | C Brad | 33 | K3 |
| Birdlip | Gloucs | 22 | A8 |
| Birkenhead | Wirral | 32 | C7 |
| Birmingham | Birm | 22 | B2 |
| Birstall | Leics | 30 | C8 |
| Birtley | Gatesd | 43 | K6 |
| Bishop Auckland | Dur | 38 | C1 |
| Bishop's Castle | Shrops | 21 | G2 |
| Bishop's Cleeve | Gloucs | 22 | A7 |
| Bishop's Frome | Herefs | 21 | K5 |
| Bishops Lydeard | Somset | 12 | C7 |
| Bishop's Stortford | Herts | 16 | D5 |
| Bishopsteignton | Devon | 6 | C4 |
| Bishopston | Swans | 19 | J7 |
| Bishopstone | Swindn | 13 | M3 |
| Bishop Sutton | BaNES | 13 | G5 |
| Bishop's Waltham | Hants | 8 | F4 |
| Bitchfield | Lincs | 30 | F6 |
| Bitton | S Glos | 13 | G4 |
| Blaby | Leics | 22 | F1 |
| Blackbrook | Staffs | 28 | E6 |
| Blackburn | Bl w D | 32 | F4 |
| Blackford | P & K | 50 | E6 |
| Blackmill | Brdgnd | 19 | M7 |
| Blackpool | Bpool | 32 | C3 |
| Black Torrington | Devon | 4 | D6 |
| Blackwater | Hants | 14 | F7 |
| Blackwater | IoW | 8 | F6 |
| Blackwaterfoot | N Ayrs | 44 | C5 |
| Blackwood | Caerph | 12 | C2 |
| Blackwood | S Lans | 45 | L4 |
| Bladon | Oxon | 14 | C3 |
| Blaenau Ffestiniog | Gwynd | 26 | F5 |
| Blaenavon | Torfn | 12 | D1 |
| Blaengarw | Brdgnd | 19 | L6 |
| Blaenporth | Cerdgn | 18 | F2 |
| Blagdon | N Som | 12 | F5 |
| Blair Atholl | P & K | 54 | C7 |
| Blairgowrie | P & K | 51 | G3 |
| Blairmore | Ag & B | 49 | K5 |
| Blakeney | Gloucs | 13 | G1 |
| Blakesley | Nhants | 23 | G5 |
| Blanchland | Nthumb | 43 | G6 |
| Blandford Forum | Dorset | 7 | L2 |
| Blanefield | Stirlg | 50 | B8 |
| Blaxton | Donc | 34 | D6 |
| Blaydon | Gatesd | 43 | J5 |
| Bleadney | Somset | 12 | F6 |
| Bleadon | N Som | 12 | E5 |
| Blean | Kent | 11 | J3 |
| Bleddfa | Powys | 20 | F4 |
| Bletchingley | Surrey | 10 | B3 |
| Bletchley | M Keyn | 23 | J6 |
| Bletsoe | Bed | 23 | K4 |
| Blewbury | Oxon | 14 | C5 |
| Blickling | Norfk | 25 | J3 |
| Blidworth | Notts | 30 | C4 |
| Blindley Heath | Surrey | 10 | C4 |
| Blisland | Cnwll | 3 | G4 |
| Bloxham | Oxon | 22 | E6 |
| Blubberhouses | N York | 38 | B7 |
| Blue Anchor | Somset | 5 | J3 |
| Blyth | Nthumb | 43 | K4 |
| Blyton | Lincs | 34 | E7 |
| Boat of Garten | Highld | 54 | D3 |
| Boddam | Abers | 61 | H5 |
| Bodfari | Denbgs | 27 | J3 |
| Bodfuan | Gwynd | 26 | C6 |
| Bodiam | E Susx | 10 | F5 |
| Bodmin | Cnwll | 3 | G4 |
| Bognor Regis | W Susx | 9 | J6 |
| Bollington | Ches E | 29 | G3 |
| Bolney | W Susx | 10 | B6 |
| Bolsover | Derbys | 29 | L3 |
| Bolton | Bolton | 32 | F6 |
| Bolton Abbey | N York | 33 | J2 |
| Bolton-le-Sands | Lancs | 37 | H6 |
| Bolventor | Cnwll | 3 | H3 |
| Bonar Bridge | Highld | 64 | C8 |
| Bonchester Bridge | Border | 42 | D1 |
| Bo'ness | Falk | 46 | A2 |
| Bonnyrigg | Mdloth | 46 | D4 |
| Bontnewydd | Gwynd | 26 | D4 |
| Bonvilston | V Glam | 12 | B4 |
| Boot | Cumb | 36 | E3 |
| Bootle | Cumb | 36 | E4 |
| Bootle | Sefton | 32 | C7 |
| Bordeaux | Guern | 6 | b1 |
| Boreham Street | E Susx | 10 | E6 |
| Borehamwood | Herts | 15 | J4 |
| Boroughbridge | N York | 38 | D6 |
| Borough Green | Kent | 10 | E3 |
| Borrowash | Derbys | 29 | L6 |
| Borth | Cerdgn | 20 | A2 |
| Borth-y-Gest | Gwynd | 26 | E6 |
| Boscastle | Cnwll | 3 | G2 |
| Bosham | W Susx | 9 | H5 |
| Bosherston | Pembks | 18 | D6 |
| Boston | Lincs | 31 | J5 |
| Boston Spa | Leeds | 34 | B3 |
| Botesdale | Suffk | 25 | H7 |
| Bothel | Cumb | 41 | M7 |
| Bottesford | Leics | 30 | E6 |
| Bottesford | N Linc | 34 | F6 |
| Bough Beech | Kent | 10 | D4 |
| Boughton Street | Kent | 11 | H3 |
| Boulmer | Nthumb | 47 | M7 |
| Bourne | Lincs | 31 | G7 |
| Bourne End | Bucks | 14 | F5 |
| Bournemouth | Bmouth | 8 | B6 |
| Bourton | Shrops | 21 | K2 |
| Bourton-on-the-Water | Gloucs | 22 | C7 |
| Bovey Tracey | Devon | 6 | B4 |
| Bowes | Dur | 37 | M3 |
| Bowmore | Ag & B | 48 | C7 |
| Bowness-on-Solway | Cumb | 41 | M5 |
| Bowness-on-Windermere | Cumb | 37 | G4 |
| Box | Wilts | 13 | J4 |
| Boxford | Suffk | 17 | H4 |
| Bozeat | Nhants | 23 | J4 |
| Bracadale | Highld | 56 | D5 |
| Brackley | Nhants | 23 | G6 |
| Bracknell | Br For | 14 | F6 |
| Bradford | C Brad | 33 | K4 |
| Bradford-on-Avon | Wilts | 13 | J5 |
| Brading | IoW | 8 | F6 |
| Bradwell | Derbys | 29 | J2 |
| Bradwell-on-Sea | Essex | 17 | H6 |
| Bradworthy | Devon | 4 | C6 |
| Brae | Shet | 61 | b4 |
| Braemar | Abers | 54 | E5 |
| Braeswick | Ork | 65 | d2 |
| Braidwood | S Lans | 45 | L3 |
| Brailsford | Derbys | 29 | J5 |
| Braintree | Essex | 16 | F5 |
| Braithwaite | Cumb | 36 | F2 |
| Bramdean | Hants | 8 | F3 |
| Bramfield | Suffk | 25 | K7 |
| Bramham | Leeds | 34 | B3 |
| Bramhope | Leeds | 33 | L3 |
| Bramley | Hants | 14 | D7 |
| Bramley | Surrey | 9 | K2 |
| Brampton | Cambs | 23 | M3 |
| Brampton | Cumb | 42 | D5 |
| Bramshaw | Hants | 8 | D4 |
| Brancaster | Norfk | 24 | E2 |
| Brandesburton | E R Yk | 35 | H3 |
| Brandon | Dur | 43 | J7 |
| Brandon | Suffk | 24 | E6 |
| Brandon | Warwks | 22 | E3 |
| Branscombe | Devon | 6 | E5 |
| Bransgore | Hants | 8 | C6 |
| Branston | Lincs | 30 | F3 |
| Branthwaite | Cumb | 36 | D2 |
| Brassington | Derbys | 29 | J4 |
| Brasted | Kent | 10 | D3 |
| Bratton | Wilts | 13 | J6 |
| Bratton Clovelly | Devon | 3 | K2 |
| Bratton Fleming | Devon | 4 | F4 |
| Braughing | Herts | 16 | C5 |
| Braunton | Devon | 4 | E4 |
| Brayford | Devon | 4 | F4 |
| Breascleit | W Isls | 62 | g3 |
| Breasclete | W Isls | 62 | g3 |
| Brechfa | Carmth | 19 | H4 |
| Brechin | Angus | 55 | J7 |
| Brecon | Powys | 20 | E7 |
| Brede | E Susx | 11 | G6 |
| Bredenbury | Herefs | 21 | K5 |
| Bredhurst | Kent | 10 | F3 |
| Bredon | Worcs | 22 | A6 |
| Bredwardine | Herefs | 21 | G6 |
| Brendon | Devon | 5 | G3 |
| Brent Knoll | Somset | 12 | E6 |
| Brentwood | Essex | 16 | E7 |
| Brenzett | Kent | 11 | H5 |
| Brereton Green | Ches E | 28 | E4 |
| Brewood | Staffs | 28 | F8 |
| Bride | IoM | 36 | c1 |
| Bridestowe | Devon | 3 | L2 |
| Bridge | Kent | 11 | J3 |
| Bridgend | Ag & B | 48 | C6 |
| Bridgend | Brdgnd | 19 | L7 |
| Bridge of Allan | Stirlg | 50 | B6 |
| Bridge of Cally | P & K | 51 | G2 |
| Bridge of Earn | P & K | 51 | G5 |
| Bridge of Orchy | Ag & B | 53 | K6 |
| Bridge of Weir | Rens | 49 | M6 |
| Bridgnorth | Shrops | 21 | L2 |
| Bridgwater | Somset | 12 | D7 |
| Bridlington | E R Yk | 39 | L6 |
| Bridport | Dorset | 7 | H3 |
| Brierfield | Lancs | 33 | H3 |
| Brigg | N Linc | 35 | G6 |
| Brigham | Cumb | 41 | L8 |
| Brighouse | Calder | 33 | K4 |
| Brighstone | IoW | 8 | E7 |
| Brightlingsea | Essex | 17 | J5 |
| Brighton | Br & H | 10 | B7 |
| Brigstock | Nhants | 23 | K2 |
| Brinklow | Warwks | 22 | E3 |
| Brinkworth | Wilts | 13 | K3 |
| Brinyan | Ork | 65 | c3 |
| Bristol | Bristl | 13 | G4 |
| Brixham | Torbay | 6 | C6 |
| Brixton | Devon | 3 | L5 |
| Brixton | Gt Lon | 15 | K6 |
| Brixworth | Nhants | 23 | H3 |
| Broad Blunsdon | Swindn | 13 | L3 |
| Broadbridge Heath | W Susx | 9 | L3 |
| Broad Chalke | Wilts | 13 | K8 |
| Broadclyst | Devon | 6 | D3 |
| Broadford | Highld | 56 | F6 |
| Broad Haven | Pembks | 18 | C5 |
| Broadstairs | Kent | 11 | L2 |
| Broadway | Worcs | 22 | C6 |
| Broadwindsor | Dorset | 7 | G2 |
| Brockdish | Norfk | 25 | J7 |
| Brockenhurst | Hants | 8 | D5 |
| Brockford Street | Suffk | 17 | J1 |
| Brockworth | Gloucs | 21 | M8 |
| Brodick | N Ayrs | 44 | D4 |
| Brome | Suffk | 25 | H7 |
| Bromfield | Shrops | 21 | J3 |
| Bromham | Beds | 23 | K5 |
| Bromley | Gt Lon | 10 | C2 |
| Brompton-by-Sawdon | N York | 39 | J5 |
| Brompton Regis | Somset | 5 | H4 |
| Bromsgrove | Worcs | 22 | A3 |
| Bromyard | Herefs | 21 | K5 |
| Bronllys | Powys | 20 | F6 |
| Brooke | Norfk | 25 | K6 |
| Brookland | Kent | 11 | H5 |
| Brookmans Park | Herts | 15 | J4 |
| Broomhill | Nthumb | 43 | K2 |
| Brora | Highld | 64 | F7 |
| Broseley | Shrops | 21 | K1 |
| Brotherton | N York | 34 | B4 |
| Brotton | R & Cl | 39 | G2 |
| Brough | Cumb | 37 | K2 |
| Brough | E R Yk | 34 | F4 |
| Broughton | Border | 46 | B6 |
| Broughton | N Linc | 34 | F6 |
| Broughton-in-Furness | Cumb | 36 | F5 |
| Broughton Moor | Cumb | 41 | K7 |
| Broughton Poggs | Oxon | 13 | M2 |
| Brownhills | Wsall | 29 | H8 |
| Broxburn | W Loth | 46 | B3 |
| Broxted | Essex | 16 | D5 |
| Brundall | Norfk | 25 | K5 |
| Bruton | Somset | 13 | G7 |
| Brynamman | Carmth | 19 | K5 |
| Bryncrug | Gwynd | 20 | A1 |
| Brynmawr | Blae G | 12 | C1 |
| Bubwith | E R Yk | 34 | D3 |
| Buchlyvie | Stirlg | 50 | B7 |
| Buckden | Cambs | 23 | M4 |
| Buckden | N York | 37 | M5 |
| Buckfastleigh | Devon | 6 | B5 |
| Buckhaven | Fife | 51 | H6 |
| Buckhorn Weston | Dorset | 13 | H8 |
| Buckie | Moray | 60 | B3 |
| Buckingham | Bucks | 23 | G6 |
| Buckland | Herts | 16 | C4 |
| Bucklers Hard | Hants | 8 | E5 |
| Buckley | Flints | 27 | L4 |
| Bucklow Hill | Ches E | 28 | E2 |
| Buckminster | Leics | 30 | E7 |
| Bude | Cnwll | 4 | B6 |
| Budleigh Salterton | Devon | 6 | D4 |
| Bugle | Cnwll | 2 | F5 |
| Builth Wells | Powys | 20 | E5 |
| Bulford | Wilts | 13 | K7 |
| Bulkington | Warwks | 22 | E2 |
| Bulphan | Thurr | 16 | E8 |
| Bulwick | Nhants | 23 | K2 |
| Bunessan | Ag & B | 48 | C2 |
| Bungay | Suffk | 25 | K6 |
| Bunny | Notts | 30 | C6 |
| Buntingford | Herts | 16 | C4 |
| Bunwell | Norfk | 25 | H6 |
| Burbage | Wilts | 13 | M5 |
| Bures | Essex | 17 | G4 |
| Burford | Oxon | 13 | M1 |
| Burgess Hill | W Susx | 10 | B6 |
| Burgh by Sands | Cumb | 42 | B6 |
| Burgh Castle | Norfk | 25 | L5 |
| Burghead | Moray | 59 | J3 |
| Burghfield | W Berk | 14 | D6 |
| Burgh le Marsh | Lincs | 31 | K4 |
| Burley | Hants | 8 | C5 |
| Burleydam | Ches E | 28 | D5 |
| Burley in Wharfedale | C Brad | 33 | K3 |
| Burlton | Shrops | 28 | C7 |
| Burneston | N York | 38 | C5 |
| Burnham Market | Norfk | 24 | F2 |
| Burnham-on-Crouch | Essex | 17 | H7 |
| Burnham-on-Sea | Somset | 12 | D6 |
| Burnham Overy Staithe | Norfk | 24 | F2 |
| Burnley | Lancs | 33 | G4 |
| Burnopfield | Dur | 43 | J6 |
| Burntisland | Fife | 46 | C2 |
| Burntwood | Staffs | 29 | H8 |
| Burravoe | Shet | 61 | d3 |
| Burrelton | P & K | 51 | G3 |
| Burrington | Devon | 4 | F5 |
| Burry Port | Carmth | 19 | H6 |
| Burscough Bridge | Lancs | 32 | D5 |
| Bursledon | Hants | 8 | E5 |
| Burton | Ches W | 27 | L3 |
| Burton Agnes | E R Yk | 39 | K6 |
| Burton Bradstock | Dorset | 7 | H3 |
| Burton Fleming | E R Yk | 39 | K6 |
| Burton-in-Kendal | Cumb | 37 | H5 |
| Burton Joyce | Notts | 30 | C5 |

| | | |
|---|---|---|
| Burton Latimer | | |
| Nhants | 23 | J3 |
| Burton upon | | |
| Stather N Linc | 34 | F5 |
| Burton upon Trent | | |
| Staffs | 29 | J7 |
| Burwash E Susx | 10 | E5 |
| Burwell Cambs | 16 | E1 |
| Burwick Ork | 65 | c6 |
| Bury Bury | 33 | G5 |
| Bury St Edmunds | | |
| Suffk | 17 | G2 |
| Bushey Herts | 15 | H4 |
| Butley Suffk | 17 | L3 |
| Buttermere Cumb | 36 | E2 |
| Butterwick Lincs | 31 | J5 |
| Buttington Powys | 27 | K8 |
| Buxted E Susx | 10 | D6 |
| Buxton Derbys | 29 | H3 |
| Bwlch Powys | 20 | F7 |
| Byfleet Surrey | 15 | H7 |
| Bylchau Conwy | 27 | H4 |
| Byrness Nthumb | 42 | F2 |

**C**

| | | |
|---|---|---|
| Cadgwith Cnwll | 2 | D8 |
| Caerleon Newpt | 12 | E3 |
| Caernarfon Gwynd | 26 | D4 |
| Caerphilly Caerph | 12 | C3 |
| Caersws Powys | 20 | E2 |
| Caerwent Mons | 12 | F3 |
| Caerwys Flints | 27 | J3 |
| Cairndow Ag & B | 49 | K3 |
| Cairnryan D & G | 40 | B5 |
| Caister-on-Sea Norfk | 25 | L5 |
| Caistor Lincs | 35 | H6 |
| Caldbeck Cumb | 42 | B7 |
| Caldecott Rutlnd | 23 | J2 |
| Calder Bridge Cumb | 36 | D3 |
| Caldercruix N Lans | 45 | L2 |
| Caldicot Mons | 12 | F3 |
| Calfsound Ork | 65 | d2 |
| Calgary Ag & B | 52 | B5 |
| Callander Stirlg | 50 | B6 |
| Callington Cnwll | 3 | J4 |
| Calne Wilts | 13 | K4 |
| Calshot Hants | 8 | E5 |
| Calverton Notts | 30 | C5 |
| Calvine P & K | 54 | C7 |
| Camber E Susx | 11 | H6 |
| Camberley Surrey | 14 | F7 |
| Cambo Nthumb | 43 | H4 |
| Camborne Cnwll | 2 | C6 |
| Cambourne Cambs | 16 | B2 |
| Cambridge Cambs | 16 | C2 |
| Cambridge Gloucs | 13 | H2 |
| Cambuslang S Lans | 45 | K2 |
| Camden Town Gt Lon | 15 | K5 |
| Camelford Cnwll | 3 | G3 |
| Campbeltown Ag & B | 44 | B5 |
| Candlesby Lincs | 31 | K3 |
| Cannich Highld | 58 | C6 |
| Cannington Somset | 12 | D7 |
| Cannock Staffs | 29 | G8 |
| Canonbie D & G | 42 | C4 |
| Canterbury Kent | 11 | J3 |
| Canvey Island Essex | 16 | F8 |
| Caoles Ag & B | 48 | b2 |
| Capel Surrey | 9 | L2 |
| Capel Bangor Cerdgn | 20 | B3 |
| Capel Curig Conwy | 26 | F4 |
| Capel St Mary Suffk | 17 | J4 |
| Caputh P & K | 50 | F3 |
| Carbost Highld | 56 | D6 |
| Cardiff Cardif | 12 | C4 |
| Cardigan Cerdgn | 18 | E2 |
| Cardington Bed | 23 | L5 |
| Cardross Ag & B | 49 | L5 |
| Carew Pembks | 18 | D6 |
| Carfraemill Border | 46 | F4 |
| Carhampton Somset | 5 | J3 |
| Cark Cumb | 37 | G5 |
| Carlabhagh W Isls | 62 | g3 |
| Carlisle Cumb | 42 | C6 |
| Carlops Border | 46 | C4 |
| Carloway W Isls | 62 | g3 |
| Carlton N York | 34 | D4 |
| Carlton N York | 38 | A5 |
| Carlton-on-Trent | | |
| Notts | 30 | D4 |
| Carluke S Lans | 45 | L3 |
| Carmarthen Carmth | 19 | G4 |
| Carnaby E R Yk | 39 | K6 |
| Carnforth Lancs | 37 | H6 |
| Carno Powys | 20 | D2 |
| Carnon Downs Cnwll | 2 | C6 |
| Carnoustie Angus | 51 | K4 |
| Carnwath S Lans | 46 | A5 |
| Carradale Ag & B | 44 | C4 |

| | | |
|---|---|---|
| Carrbridge Highld | 59 | H6 |
| Carrefour Jersey | 7 | b1 |
| Carrick Castle Ag & B | 49 | K4 |
| Carronbridge D & G | 41 | J3 |
| Carrutherstown | | |
| D & G | 41 | L5 |
| Carsphairn D & G | 40 | F3 |
| Carstairs S Lans | 45 | M3 |
| Carterton Oxon | 14 | A3 |
| Cartmel Cumb | 37 | G5 |
| Castel Guern | 6 | a2 |
| Casterton Cumb | 37 | J5 |
| Castle Acre Norfk | 24 | F4 |
| Castlebay W Isls | 62 | b14 |
| Castle Carrock Cumb | 42 | D6 |
| Castle Cary Somset | 13 | G7 |
| Castle Donington | | |
| Leics | 29 | L6 |
| Castle Douglas D & G | 41 | H5 |
| Castleford Wakefd | 34 | B4 |
| Castlemartin Pembks | 18 | C6 |
| Castle Rising Norfk | 24 | D4 |
| Castleside Dur | 43 | H6 |
| Castleton Derbys | 29 | H2 |
| Castleton N York | 39 | G3 |
| Castleton Newpt | 12 | D3 |
| Castletown Highld | 65 | H2 |
| Castletown IoM | 36 | b4 |
| Caterham Surrey | 10 | C3 |
| Catfield Norfk | 25 | K4 |
| Caton Lancs | 37 | H6 |
| Catrine E Ayrs | 45 | J5 |
| Catsfield E Susx | 10 | F6 |
| Catterick N York | 38 | C4 |
| Caunton Notts | 30 | D4 |
| Cawdor Highld | 59 | G4 |
| Cawsand Cnwll | 3 | K5 |
| Caxton Cambs | 16 | B2 |
| Caythorpe Lincs | 30 | F5 |
| Cayton N York | 39 | K5 |
| Cemaes IoA | 26 | C1 |
| Cemmaes Road | | |
| Powys | 20 | C1 |
| Ceres Fife | 51 | J5 |
| Cerne Abbas Dorset | 7 | J2 |
| Cerrigydrudion | | |
| Conwy | 27 | H5 |
| Chadderton Oldham | 33 | H6 |
| Chadlington Oxon | 14 | B2 |
| Chagford Devon | 6 | A3 |
| Chale IoW | 8 | E7 |
| Chalfont St Giles | | |
| Bucks | 15 | G4 |
| Chalfont St Peter | | |
| Bucks | 15 | G4 |
| Chalford Gloucs | 13 | J2 |
| Challacombe Devon | 4 | F3 |
| Challock Kent | 11 | H3 |
| Chandler's Ford | | |
| Hants | 8 | E4 |
| Chapel-en-le-Frith | | |
| Derbys | 29 | H2 |
| Chapel St Leonards | | |
| Lincs | 31 | L3 |
| Chapeltown Sheff | 34 | A4 |
| Chapmanslade Wilts | 13 | J6 |
| Chard Somset | 6 | F2 |
| Charing Kent | 11 | H4 |
| Charlbury Oxon | 14 | B2 |
| Charlecote Warwks | 22 | D5 |
| Charlestown of | | |
| Aberlour Moray | 59 | L5 |
| Charlton Kings | | |
| Gloucs | 22 | A7 |
| Charlton Marshall | | |
| Dorset | 7 | L2 |
| Charlwood Surrey | 10 | B4 |
| Charmouth Dorset | 7 | G3 |
| Chartham Kent | 11 | J3 |
| Chatburn Lancs | 33 | G3 |
| Chatham Medway | 10 | F2 |
| Chatteris Cambs | 24 | B7 |
| Chatton Nthumb | 47 | K6 |
| Chawleigh Devon | 4 | F6 |
| Chawton Hants | 9 | G3 |
| Cheadle Staffs | 29 | G5 |
| Cheadle Stockp | 33 | H7 |
| Cheddar Somset | 12 | F5 |
| Cheddleton Staffs | 29 | G5 |
| Chelford Ches E | 28 | F3 |
| Chelmsford Essex | 16 | F6 |
| Cheltenham Gloucs | 22 | A7 |
| Chepstow Mons | 12 | F3 |
| Cheriton Hants | 8 | F3 |
| Cheriton Fitzpaine | | |
| Devon | 5 | H6 |
| Chertsey Surrey | 15 | G6 |
| Chesham Bucks | 15 | G4 |
| Cheshunt Herts | 15 | K4 |
| Chester Ches W | 28 | B3 |
| Chesterfield Derbys | 29 | K3 |
| Chester-le-Street Dur | 43 | K6 |

| | | |
|---|---|---|
| Chew Magna BaNES | 13 | G5 |
| Chewton Mendip | | |
| Somset | 13 | G6 |
| Chicheley M Keyn | 23 | J5 |
| Chichester W Susx | 9 | H5 |
| Chickerell Dorset | 7 | J4 |
| Chicklade Wilts | 13 | J7 |
| Chiddingfold Surrey | 9 | J3 |
| Chieveley W Berk | 14 | C6 |
| Chigwell Essex | 16 | C7 |
| Childer Thornton | | |
| Ches W | 28 | B3 |
| Chilham Kent | 11 | J3 |
| Chillington Devon | 6 | B7 |
| Chilmark Wilts | 13 | K7 |
| Chilsworthy Devon | 4 | C6 |
| Chilton Foliat Wilts | 14 | A6 |
| Chineham Hants | 14 | D7 |
| Chinnor Oxon | 14 | E4 |
| Chippenham Cambs | 16 | E1 |
| Chippenham Wilts | 13 | J4 |
| Chipperfield Herts | 15 | G4 |
| Chipping Lancs | 32 | F3 |
| Chipping Campden | | |
| Gloucs | 22 | C6 |
| Chipping Norton | | |
| Oxon | 22 | D7 |
| Chipping Ongar | | |
| Essex | 16 | D6 |
| Chipping Sodbury | | |
| S Glos | 13 | H3 |
| Chipping Warden | | |
| Nhants | 22 | F5 |
| Chirbury Shrops | 21 | G1 |
| Chirk Wrexhm | 27 | L6 |
| Chirnside Border | 47 | J4 |
| Chiseldon Swindn | 13 | M4 |
| Chitterne Wilts | 13 | K6 |
| Chittlehamholt | | |
| Devon | 4 | F5 |
| Chobham Surrey | 15 | G7 |
| Cholderton Wilts | 8 | C2 |
| Chorley Lancs | 32 | E5 |
| Chorleywood Herts | 15 | G4 |
| Christchurch Dorset | 8 | C6 |
| Chudleigh Devon | 6 | C4 |
| Chudleigh Knighton | | |
| Devon | 6 | C4 |
| Chulmleigh Devon | 4 | F6 |
| Churchill Oxon | 14 | A2 |
| Churchstoke Powys | 21 | G2 |
| Church Stretton | | |
| Shrops | 21 | G2 |
| Churston Ferrers | | |
| Torbay | 6 | C6 |
| Churt Surrey | 9 | H3 |
| Cinderford Gloucs | 21 | K8 |
| Cirencester Gloucs | 13 | K2 |
| Clachan Ag & B | 44 | B3 |
| Clachan Highld | 56 | E5 |
| Clackmannan Clacks | 50 | E7 |
| Clacton-on-Sea Essex | 17 | J5 |
| Clanfield Oxon | 14 | A4 |
| Claonaig Ag & B | 44 | C3 |
| Clapham Bed | 23 | K5 |
| Clapham N York | 37 | K6 |
| Clare Suffk | 16 | F3 |
| Clatt Abers | 60 | C6 |
| Claverdon Warwks | 22 | C4 |
| Clavering Essex | 16 | D4 |
| Clawton Devon | 4 | C7 |
| Clay Cross Derbys | 29 | K4 |
| Claydon Suffk | 17 | J3 |
| Cleator Moor Cumb | 36 | D2 |
| Cleethorpes NE Lin | 35 | J6 |
| Cleeve N Som | 12 | F5 |
| Cleeve Hill Gloucs | 22 | B7 |
| Cleobury Mortimer | | |
| Shrops | 21 | K3 |
| Cleobury North | | |
| Shrops | 21 | K3 |
| Clevedon N Som | 12 | E4 |
| Cleveleys Lancs | 32 | C3 |
| Cley next the Sea | | |
| Norfk | 25 | G2 |
| Cliffe Medway | 10 | F2 |
| Cliffe N York | 34 | D4 |
| Cliffe Woods Medway | 10 | F2 |
| Clifton Cumb | 37 | H2 |
| Clifton upon Teme | | |
| Worcs | 21 | L4 |
| Climping W Susx | 9 | K5 |
| Clitheroe Lancs | 33 | G3 |
| Clola Abers | 61 | G5 |
| Clophill C Beds | 23 | L6 |
| Closworth Somset | 7 | H2 |
| Cloughton N York | 39 | J4 |
| Clova Angus | 55 | G6 |
| Clovelly Devon | 4 | C5 |
| Clovenfords Border | 46 | E6 |
| Clowne Derbys | 30 | B3 |
| Clows Top Worcs | 21 | L3 |

| | | |
|---|---|---|
| Clun Shrops | 21 | G3 |
| Clydach Swans | 19 | J6 |
| Clydebank W Duns | 45 | H2 |
| Clynder Ag & B | 49 | K5 |
| Clynnog-fawr Gwynd | 26 | D5 |
| Clyro Powys | 20 | F6 |
| Clyst St Mary Devon | 6 | D3 |
| Coalport Wrekin | 21 | K1 |
| Coalville Leics | 29 | L7 |
| Coatbridge N Lans | 45 | K2 |
| Cobham Kent | 10 | E2 |
| Cockburnspath | | |
| Border | 47 | H3 |
| Cockermouth Cumb | 41 | L8 |
| Cocking W Susx | 9 | J4 |
| Coddenham Suffk | 17 | J2 |
| Codford St Mary | | |
| Wilts | 13 | K7 |
| Codicote Herts | 15 | J3 |
| Codnor Derbys | 29 | L5 |
| Codsall Staffs | 21 | M1 |
| Coedpoeth Wrexhm | 27 | L5 |
| Coggeshall Essex | 17 | G5 |
| Colchester Essex | 17 | H5 |
| Cold Ash W Berk | 14 | C6 |
| Cold Ashby Nhants | 23 | G3 |
| Cold Ashton S Glos | 13 | H4 |
| Coldingham Border | 47 | J3 |
| Cold Norton Essex | 17 | G7 |
| Coldstream Border | 47 | H5 |
| Coleford Gloucs | 13 | G1 |
| Colerne Wilts | 13 | J4 |
| Coleshill Warwks | 22 | C2 |
| Colintraive Ag & B | 49 | J6 |
| Collier's End Herts | 15 | K2 |
| Collieston Abers | 61 | G6 |
| Collingbourne Ducis | | |
| Wilts | 13 | M6 |
| Collingham Leeds | 34 | B3 |
| Colmonell S Ayrs | 40 | C3 |
| Colne Lancs | 33 | H3 |
| Colne Engaine Essex | 17 | G4 |
| Coln St Aldwyns | | |
| Gloucs | 13 | L2 |
| Colpy Abers | 60 | D6 |
| Colsterworth Lincs | 30 | F7 |
| Coltishall Norfk | 25 | J4 |
| Colwell Nthumb | 43 | G4 |
| Colwyn Bay Conwy | 27 | G2 |
| Colyford Devon | 6 | F3 |
| Colyton Devon | 6 | F3 |
| Combe Martin Devon | 4 | E3 |
| Compton Surrey | 9 | J2 |
| Compton W Berk | 14 | C5 |
| Comrie P & K | 50 | D5 |
| Congleton Ches E | 28 | F4 |
| Congresbury N Som | 12 | E5 |
| Coningsby Lincs | 31 | H4 |
| Conington Cambs | 23 | M2 |
| Conisbrough Donc | 34 | C6 |
| Coniston Cumb | 36 | F4 |
| Connah's Quay Flints | 27 | L3 |
| Connel Ag & B | 52 | F7 |
| Conon Bridge Highld | 58 | E4 |
| Consett Dur | 43 | H6 |
| Constantine Cnwll | 2 | D7 |
| Contin Highld | 58 | D4 |
| Conwy Conwy | 27 | G3 |
| Cookham W & M | 14 | F5 |
| Coolham W Susx | 9 | L4 |
| Coombe Bissett Wilts | 8 | B3 |
| Coombe Hill Gloucs | 21 | M7 |
| Copdock Suffk | 17 | J3 |
| Copford Green Essex | 17 | G5 |
| Copley Dur | 38 | B2 |
| Copplestone Devon | 5 | G6 |
| Copthorne W Susx | 10 | B4 |
| Corbière Jersey | 7 | a2 |
| Corbridge Nthumb | 43 | G5 |
| Corby Nhants | 23 | J2 |
| Corby Glen Lincs | 30 | F7 |
| Corfe Somset | 6 | F1 |
| Corfe Castle Dorset | 7 | M4 |
| Corgarff Abers | 55 | G2 |
| Cornhill-on-Tweed | | |
| Nthumb | 47 | H5 |
| Cornwood Devon | 3 | L5 |
| Corpach Highld | 53 | H3 |
| Corrie N Ayrs | 44 | D4 |
| Corris Gwynd | 26 | F8 |
| Corsham Wilts | 13 | J4 |
| Corston Wilts | 13 | J3 |
| Corton Suffk | 25 | M6 |
| Corwen Denbgs | 27 | J5 |
| Coryton Thurr | 16 | F8 |
| Cosby Leics | 22 | F2 |
| Cotebrook Ches W | 28 | D3 |
| Cotherstone Dur | 38 | A2 |
| Cottenham Cambs | 16 | C1 |
| Cottered Herts | 16 | B4 |
| Cottingham E R Yk | 35 | G4 |
| Coulport Ag & B | 49 | K5 |

Coulter S Lans .........46 B6
Countesthorpe Leics ...23 G2
Coupar Angus P & K ...51 G3
Cove Highld ..............62 D8
Coventry Covtry .........22 E3
Coverack Cnwll ............2 D8
Cowbit Lincs .............31 H7
Cowbridge V Glam ......12 B4
Cowden Kent .............10 D4
Cowdenbeath Fife .......51 G7
Cowes IoW ..................8 E6
Cowfold W Susx ...........9 L4
Cowling N York ..........33 J3
Coxheath Kent ...........10 F3
Coxwold N York .........38 E5
Coylton S Ayrs ...........45 H6
Coylumbridge Highld ...54 D3
Crackington Haven
    Cnwll ...................4 B7
Cracoe N York ...........37 M7
Crafthole Cnwll ...........3 J5
Craigellachie Moray .....59 L5
Craighouse Ag & B .....48 D6
Craignure Ag & B .......52 E6
Craigrothie Fife ..........51 J5
Crail Fife ..................51 L6
Crailing Border ..........47 G7
Cramlington Nthumb ...43 K4
Cranborne Dorset ........8 B4
Cranbrook Kent ..........10 F5
Cranfield C Beds ........23 K6
Cranham Gloucs .........21 M8
Cranleigh Surrey ..........9 K2
Cranshaws Border ......47 C4
Crarae Ag & B ...........49 H4
Craster Nthumb .........47 M7
Crathie Abers ............54 F5
Crathorne N York .......38 E3
Craven Arms Shrops ...21 H3
Crawford S Lans .........46 A7
Crawfordjohn S Lans ...45 M5
Crawley W Susx .........10 B5
Crawley Down
    W Susx ...............10 B4
Creag Ghoraidh
    W Isls .................62 c10
Creagorry W Isls ........62 c10
Credenhill Herefs .......21 H6
Crediton Devon ...........5 G7
Creetown D & G .........40 F6
Cregneash IoM ..........36 a4
Cressage Shrops ........21 K1
Crewe Ches E ...........28 E4
Crewkerne Somset ......7 G2
Crianlarich Stirlg .......53 K7
Criccieth Gwynd ........26 D6
Crickhowell Powys .....20 F7
Cricklade Wilts ..........13 L3
Crieff P & K ..............50 D5
Crimond Abers ..........61 H4
Crinan Ag & B ...........49 G4
Cringleford Norfk .......25 J5
Crockernwell Devon .....6 B3
Crockerford D & G ......41 J4
Croglin Cumb ............42 D6
Cromarty Highld ........59 G3
Cromdale Highld ........59 J6
Cromer Norfk ............25 J2
Cromford Derbys ........29 K4
Cromwell Notts .........30 E4
Crook Dur .................43 J7
Crooklands Cumb .......37 H5
Cropredy Oxon ...........22 F5
Cropton N York .........39 G4
Crosby IoM ...............36 b3
Crosby Sefton ...........32 C6
Crossford Fife ...........46 B2
Crossford S Lans ........45 L3
Cross Hands Carmth ...19 H5
Crosshill S Ayrs .........45 G6
Cross in Hand E Susx ..10 D6
Crosskeys Caerph .......12 D3
Crossmichael D & G ...41 H5
Crossway Green
    Worcs .................21 M4
Crosthwaite Cumb ......37 G4
Crowborough E Susx ..10 D5
Crowcombe Somset .....5 K4
Crowhurst E Susx .......10 F6
Crowland Lincs ..........31 H8
Crowle N Linc ...........34 E5
Crowthorne Wokham ..14 F7
Croxton Kerrial Leics ..30 E6
Croy Highld ..............59 G4
Croyde Devon .............4 D4
Croydon Gt Lon .........15 K7
Cruden Bay Abers ......61 H5
Crudgington Wrekin ...28 D7
Crudwell Wilts ..........13 K3
Crynant Neath ..........19 K5
Cuckfield W Susx ........10 B5
Cuckney Notts ...........30 C3

Cuddington Ches W ....28 D3
Cudworth Barns .........34 B6
Cuffley Herts ............15 K4
Culgaith Cumb ..........37 J1
Cullen Moray .............60 C3
Cullompton Devon .......5 J6
Culmstock Devon .........5 K6
Cumbernauld N Lans ..45 L1
Cuminestown Abers ...60 E4
Cummertrees D & G ...41 L5
Cumnock E Ayrs ........45 J5
Cumnor Oxon ............14 C4
Cumrew Cumb ...........42 D6
Cupar Fife ................51 J5
Currie C Edin ............46 C3
Curry Rivel Somset ....12 E8
Cwmbran Torfn .........12 D2
Cwmystwyth Cerdgn ..20 C3
Cynwyl Elfed Carmth ..19 G4

**D**

Dailly S Ayrs .............40 D2
Dairsie Fife ..............51 J5
Dalbeattie D & G .......41 J5
Dalby IoM .................36 a3
Dale Pembks ............18 B5
Dalgety Bay Fife .......46 C2
Dalhalvaig Highld .......64 E3
Dalkeith Mdloth .........46 D3
Dallas Moray .............59 J4
Dalmally Ag & B ........53 J7
Dalmellington E Ayrs ..45 H7
Dalry N Ayrs .............45 G3
Dalrymple E Ayrs ......45 G6
Dalston Cumb ...........42 B6
Dalton D & G ............41 L4
Dalton-in-Furness
    Cumb ..................36 F6
Dalwhinnie Highld .....54 A3
Damerham Hants ........8 B4
Danbury Essex ..........16 F6
Darlington Darltn .......38 C2
Darras Hall Nthumb ...43 J5
Darrington Wakefd .....34 B5
Dartford Kent ...........10 D2
Dartington Devon ........6 B5
Dartmouth Devon ........6 C6
Darvel E Ayrs ............45 J4
Darwen Bl w D ..........32 F5
Datchet W & M .........15 G6
Dava Highld ..............59 H5
Davenham Ches W .....28 D3
Daventry Nhants ........23 G4
Daviot Highld ...........58 F5
Dawlish Devon ...........6 C4
Deal Kent .................11 L3
Dearham Cumb ..........41 L7
Debenham Suffk ........17 J2
Deddington Oxon .......22 F6
Dedham Essex ..........17 H4
Deeping St James
    Lincs ...................31 H8
Deeping St Nicholas
    Lincs ...................31 H7
Deganwy Conwy ........27 G2
Delabole Cnwll ...........3 G3
Denbigh Denbgs .......27 J3
Denby Dale Kirk ........33 L6
Denham Bucks ..........15 G5
Denholm Border ........46 F7
Denmead Hants ..........9 G5
Dennington Suffk .......17 K1
Denny Falk ...............50 D8
Densole Kent ............11 K4
Dent Cumb ...............37 K5
Denton Tamesd .........33 H7
Derby C Derb ...........29 K6
Derbyhaven IoM ........36 b4
Dereham Norfk ..........24 F4
Dersingham Norfk .....24 E3
Dervaig Ag & B .........52 B5
Desborough Nhants ...23 H3
Desford Leics ...........22 F1
Devil's Bridge Cerdgn ..20 B3
Devizes Wilts ...........13 K5
Dewsbury Kirk ..........33 L5
Didcot Oxon .............14 C5
Didmarton Gloucs .....13 J3
Digby Lincs ..............31 G4
Dilwyn Herefs ..........21 H5
Dinas-Mawddwy
    Gwynd ................27 G7
Dingwall Highld ........58 E4
Dinnington Rothm .....30 B2
Dippen Ag & B ..........44 C4
Diseworth Leics ........29 L7
Dishforth N York .......38 D6
Disley Ches E ...........29 G2

Diss Norfk ................25 H7
Ditchling E Susx ........10 B6
Dittisham Devon .........6 C6
Ditton Priors Shrops ..21 K2
Dobwalls Cnwll ...........3 H4
Docking Norfk ...........24 E3
Doddington Cambs ....24 B6
Doddington Kent .......11 G3
Doddington
    Nthumb ...............47 K6
Dodworth Barns ........33 L6
Dolgellau Gwynd .......26 F7
Dollar Clacks ............50 E6
Dolphinton S Lans .....46 B5
Dolton Devon .............4 E6
Dolwyddelan Conwy ..26 F5
Doncaster Donc .........34 C6
Donington Lincs ........31 H6
Dorchester Dorset ......7 K3
Dorchester-on-
    Thames Oxon ......14 D4
Dordon Warwks .........22 D1
Dores Highld ............58 E5
Dorking Surrey ...........9 L2
Dornie Highld ............57 H6
Dornoch Highld .........59 G1
Dorrington Shrops .....21 J1
Dorstone Herefs ........21 G6
Douglas IoM .............36 c3
Douglas S Lans .........45 L5
Dounby Ork ...............65 b3
Doune Stirlg .............50 C6
Dousland Devon .........3 L4
Dover Kent ...............11 L4
Doveridge Derbys ......29 H6
Dowally P & K ...........50 E3
Downderry Cnwll .........3 J5
Downham Market
    Norfk ..................24 D5
Downton Wilts ...........8 C4
Drakes Broughton
    Worcs .................22 A5
Draycott Somset .......12 F6
Drayton Norfk ...........25 J4
Drayton Oxon ...........14 C4
Driffield E R Yk .........39 J7
Drimnin Highld ..........52 C5
Droitwich Spa Worcs ..22 A4
Dronfield Derbys ........29 K3
Droxford Hants ...........8 F4
Drumbeg Highld ........63 G4
Drummore D & G .......40 C7
Drumnadrochit
    Highld .................58 D6
Drymen Stirlg ...........50 A7
Drynoch Highld .........56 D6
Duddington Nhants ....23 K1
Dudley Dudley ..........22 A2
Duffield Derbys .........29 K5
Dufftown Moray ........59 L5
Duffus Moray ............59 K3
Dulnain Bridge
    Highld .................59 H6
Dulverton Somset .......5 H4
Dumbarton W Duns ...49 M5
Dumfries D & G .........41 K4
Dunbar E Loth ..........47 G2
Dunbeath Highld .......65 H5
Dunblane Stirlg .........50 D6
Dunchurch Warwks ...22 F3
Dundee C Dund .........51 J4
Dundonald S Ayrs .....45 G4
Dundonnell Highld .....57 K1
Dundrennan D & G ....41 H6
Dunfermline Fife .......46 B2
Dunkeld P & K ..........50 F3
Dunlop E Ayrs ..........45 H3
Dunnet Highld ..........65 H2
Dunning P & K ..........50 F5
Dunoon Ag & B .........49 K5
Dunragit D & G .........40 C6
Duns Border .............47 H4
Dunscore D & G ........41 J4
Dunsfold Surrey .........9 K3
Dunsford Devon ..........6 B3
Dunsop Bridge
    Lancs ..................32 F2
Dunstable C Beds .....15 G2
Dunster Somset ..........5 H4
Duntish Dorset ...........7 K2
Dunure S Ayrs ...........44 F6
Dunvant Swans .........19 J6
Dunvegan Highld .......56 C4
Dunwich Suffk ..........25 L8
Durham Dur ..............43 K7
Durness Highld .........63 J2
Duror Highld .............53 G6
Durrington Wilts .........8 C2
Durris Abers .............55 L5
Dursley Gloucs ..........13 H2
Duxford Cambs .........55 D3
Dyce C Aber .............55 M3

**Dyffryn Ardudwy**
    Gwynd .................26 E7
Dymchurch Kent .......11 J5
Dymock Gloucs .........21 K7

**E**

Eaglesfield D & G ......42 A4
Eaglesham E Rens .....45 J3
Ealing Gt Lon ............15 J5
Earby Lancs ..............33 H3
Eardisley Herefs ........21 G5
Earith Cambs ............24 B7
Earley Wokham .........14 E6
Earls Barton Nhants ..23 J4
Earls Colne Essex ......17 G4
Earl Shilton Leics ......22 F1
Earlston Border .........46 F6
Earsham Norfk ..........25 K6
Easdale Ag & B .........48 F2
Easebourne W Susx ....9 J4
Easington Dur ...........43 L7
Easington E R Yk .......35 K5
Easingwold N York ....38 E6
East Ayton N York .....39 J5
East Barkwith Lincs ...31 H2
East Bergholt Suffk ...17 J4
Eastbourne E Susx ....10 E7
East Chinnock
    Somset ...............7 H1
Eastchurch Kent .......11 H1
East Cowes IoW ..........8 E6
East Dean E Susx ......10 D8
East Dean W Susx ......9 J4
East Goscote Leics ....30 C7
East Grinstead
    W Susx ...............10 C4
East Harling Norfk .....25 G6
East Hoathly E Susx ..10 D6
East Horsley Surrey ...15 H8
East Ilsley W Berk .....14 C5
East Kilbride S Lans ..45 J3
East Knoyle Wilts ......13 J7
East Lavant W Susx ....9 H5
Eastleigh Hants ..........8 E4
East Linton E Loth ....46 F3
East Lulworth Dorset ..7 L4
Easton Suffk .............17 K2
East Prawle Devon ......6 B7
East Preston W Susx ...9 K5
Eastriggs D & G ........42 A5
East Rudham Norfk ....24 F3
Eastry Kent ..............11 L3
East Saltoun E Loth ...46 E3
East Stoke Notts ........30 D5
East Tilbury Thurr .....10 E1
East Wittering
    W Susx ................9 H6
East Witton N York ....38 B5
Eastwood Notts .........29 L5
Eaton Socon Cambs ...23 L4
Ebbw Vale Blae G .....12 C1
Ebchester Dur ..........43 H6
Ecclefechan D & G .....41 M4
Eccles Border ...........47 H5
Eccleshall Staffs .......28 F6
Echt Abers ...............55 K4
Eckington Derbys ......29 L2
Eckington Worcs .......22 A6
Edderton Highld ........58 F2
Eddleston Border .......46 C5
Edenbridge Kent .......10 C4
Edinbane Highld ........56 D4
Edinburgh C Edin ......46 C3
Edington Lincs ..........31 H3
Edmundbyers Dur .....43 H6
Ednam Border ...........47 G6
Edwinstowe Notts .....30 C3
Edzell Angus ............55 J7
Effingham Surrey ......15 H7
Eggesford Devon ........4 F6
Eggleston Dur ..........37 M2
Egham Surrey ...........15 G6
Eglingham Nthumb ...47 K7
Eglwyswrw Pembks ...18 E3
Egremont Cumb ........36 D3
Egton Bridge N York ..39 H3
Elan Village Powys ....20 D4
Elgin Moray ..............59 K3
Elgol Highld ..............56 E7
Elham Kent ...............11 J4
Elie Fife ...................51 K6
Elkesley Notts ...........30 D3
Elkstone Gloucs ........13 K1
Elland Calder ............33 K5
Ellesmere Shrops ......28 B6
Ellesmere Port
    Ches W ................28 B3
Ellingham Norfk ........25 K6
Ellon Abers ..............61 G6

Elloughton E R Yk ........34  F4
Elmstead Market
  Essex ...................17  H5
Elsdon Nthumb .........43  G3
Elsrickle S Lans .........46  B5
Elstead Surrey ............9  J2
Elstree Herts ............15  J4
Elterwater Cumb .......37  G3
Eltisley Cambs ..........16  B2
Elton Cambs .............23  L2
Elveden Suffk ...........24  F7
Elvetham Heath Hants ..14  E7
Elvington C York ........34  D3
Elworthy Somset ..........5  J4
Ely Cambs ...............24  C7
Embleton Nthumb ......47  M7
Embo Highld .............64  E8
Empingham Rutlnd .....30  F8
Emsworth Hants ..........9  H5
Enderby Leics ...........22  F1
Enfield Gt Lon ...........15  K4
Ennerdale Bridge
  Cumb ..................36  D2
Enstone Oxon ............14  B2
Epping Essex ............16  C6
Epsom Surrey ...........15  J7
Epworth N Linc .........34  E6
Errogie Highld ..........58  E6
Errol P & K ...............51  H4
Erwood Powys ...........20  E6
Esher Surrey .............15  H7
Eskdale Green Cumb ...36  E4
Eskdalemuir D & G .....42  A3
Essendine Rutlnd .......31  G8
Essendon Herts .........15  J3
Eston R & Cl .............38  E2
Etal Nthumb .............47  J6
Etchingham E Susx .....10  F5
Eton W & M ..............15  G6
Ettington Warwks ......22  D5
Ettrick Border ...........46  D7
Ettrickbridge Border ...46  E7
Evanton Highld ..........58  E3
Evercreech Somset .....13  G7
Eversley Hants ..........14  E7
Evesham Worcs .........22  B6
Ewen Gloucs .............13  K2
Ewhurst Surrey ..........9  K2
Ewyas Harold Herefs ...21  H7
Exebridge Somset ........5  H5
Exeter Devon .............6  C3
Exford Somset ............5  H4
Exminster Devon .........6  C3
Exmouth Devon ..........6  D4
Eye C Pete ..............23  M1
Eye Suffk ................25  H7
Eyemouth Border .......47  J4
Eynsford Kent ...........10  D2
Eynsham Oxon ..........14  B3

**F**

Failsworth Oldham .....33  H6
Fairbourne Gwynd ......26  E8
Fairford Gloucs ..........13  L2
Fairlie N Ayrs ...........44  F3
Fairlight E Susx .........11  G6
Fakenham Norfk .........24  F3
Fala Mdloth .............46  E4
Faldingworth Lincs .....31  G2
Falfield S Glos ..........13  G3
Falkirk Falk ..............50  E8
Falkland Fife .............51  H6
Falmouth Cnwll ..........2  E7
Falstone Nthumb .......42  E3
Fareham Hants ...........8  F5
Faringdon Oxon .........14  A4
Farnborough Hants ....14  F7
Farnell Angus ...........51  L2
Farnham Surrey ..........9  H2
Farnham Common
  Bucks ..................15  G5
Farningham Kent .......10  D2
Far Sawrey Cumb .......37  G4
Fauldhouse W Loth ....45  M2
Faversham Kent .........11  H3
Fawley Hants .............8  E5
Fazeley Staffs ...........22  C1
Fearnan P & K ...........50  C3
Felixstowe Suffk ........17  K4
Felsted Essex ...........16  E5
Felton Nthumb ..........43  J2
Feltwell Norfk ...........24  E6
Fenny Bentley
  Derbys .................29  J3
Fenny Bridges Devon ...6  E3
Fenny Compton
  Warwks ................22  E5
Fenny Drayton Leics ...22  E1
Fenwick E Ayrs .........45  H4

Ferndown Dorset .........8  B5
Fernhill Heath Worcs ..21  M4
Fernhurst W Susx ........9  J3
Fernilee Derbys .........29  G3
Ferring W Susx ..........9  K5
Ferryhill Dur ............43  K8
Fettercairn Abers .......55  K6
Ffestiniog Gwynd .......26  F5
Filby Norfk ...............25  L4
Filey N York .............39  K5
Fincham Norfk ..........24  E5
Finchingfield Essex .....16  E4
Findhorn Moray .........59  J3
Findochty Moray ........60  C3
Findon W Susx ...........9  L5
Finedon Nhants .........23  J3
Finningham Suffk ......17  H1
Finningley Donc ........34  D6
Finstown Ork ............65  b4
Fintry Stirlg .............50  B7
Fionnphort Ag & B .....48  C2
Firle E Susx ..............10  D7
Fishbourne IoW ..........8  F6
Fishguard Pembks ......18  C3
Fittleworth W Susx ......9  K4
Fitzhead Somset ..........5  K4
Five Oaks Jersey .........7  c2
Fladdabister Shet ......61  c6
Flamborough E R Yk ..39  L6
Flamstead Herts ........15  H3
Fleet Hants ..............14  F7
Fleetwood Lancs .......32  C3
Flimby Cumb ............41  K7
Flint Flints ..............27  K3
Flitwick C Beds .........23  K6
Flixton N York ..........39  K5
Flore Nhants ............23  G4
Fochabers Moray .......59  L4
Folkestone Kent ........11  K5
Folkingham Lincs .......31  G6
Fontmell Magna
  Dorset ...................7  L1
Fontwell W Susx .........9  J5
Ford Nthumb ............47  J6
Fordcombe Kent ........10  D4
Fordingbridge Hants ....8  C4
Fordoun Abers ..........55  K6
Fordwich Kent ..........11  J3
Forest Guern .............6  a2
Forest Row E Susx .....10  C5
Forfar Angus ...........51  J2
Formby Sefton ..........32  C6
Forres Moray ...........59  J4
Fort Augustus Highld ..58  C7
Forteviot P & K .........50  F5
Forth S Lans ............45  M3
Fortingall P & K ........50  C3
Forton Lancs ...........32  E2
Fortrose Highld .........58  F4
Fortuneswell Dorset .....7  J4
Fort William Highld ....53  H4
Foston Lincs ............30  E5
Four Crosses Powys ...27  L7
Four Marks Hants ........9  G3
Fowey Cnwll ..............3  G5
Fownhope Herefs ......21  J6
Foxdale IoM ............36  b3
Foyers Highld ..........58  D7
Framlingham Suffk .....17  K2
Frampton Dorset .........7  J3
Frant E Susx ............10  E5
Fraserburgh Abers .....61  G3
Freckenham Suffk ......24  D8
Freckleton Lancs .......32  D4
Frensham Surrey .........9  H2
Freshwater IoW ..........8  D6
Fressingfield Suffk .....25  J7
Freswick Highld ........65  J2
Fridaythorpe E R Yk ...39  H7
Frilford Oxon ...........14  B4
Frinton-on-Sea Essex ..17  K5
Friockheim Angus ......51  K2
Fritton Norfk ...........25  L5
Frizington Cumb ........36  D2
Frocester Gloucs .......13  H2
Frodsham Ches W ......28  C3
Frome Somset ..........13  H6
Froxfield Wilts ..........14  A6
Funtington W Susx ......9  H5
Furnace Ag & B .........49  J4
Furness Vale Derbys ...29  G2
Fyfield Essex ...........16  D6
Fyfield Oxon ............14  B4
Fyvie Abers .............60  E4

**G**

Gailey Staffs ...........28  F8
Gainford Dur ...........38  B2
Gainsborough Lincs ....34  E7

Gairloch Highld .........57  H2
Gairlochy Highld ........53  J3
Galashiels Border .......46  E6
Galgate Lancs ..........37  H7
Galston E Ayrs ..........45  H4
Gamlingay Cambs ......16  B3
Gamston Notts ..........30  D3
Ganllwyd Gwynd .......26  F7
Garboldisham Norfk ...25  G7
Gardenstown Abers ....60  E3
Garelochhead Ag & B ..49  J6
Garforth Leeds .........34  B4
Gargrave N York ........33  H2
Garlieston D & G ........40  F6
Garlogie Abers .........55  L4
Garrigill Cumb ..........42  E7
Garstang Lancs .........32  E3
Garth Powys ............20  D5
Garvald E Loth .........46  F3
Garve Highld ...........58  C3
Gatehouse of Fleet
  D & G ..................41  G6
Gateshead Gatesd .....43  K5
Gaydon Warwks ........22  E5
Gayton Norfk ...........24  E4
Gedney Drove End
  Lincs ...................31  K6
Gedney Hill Lincs .......31  J8
Georgeham Devon .......4  D4
Gerrards Cross Bucks ..15  G5
Gifford E Loth ..........46  F3
Giggleswick N York ....37  L6
Gillingham Dorset .....13  H8
Gillingham Medway ....10  F2
Gillingham Norfk .......25  L6
Gilling West N York ....38  B3
Gills Highld .............65  J1
Gilmerton P & K ........50  E4
Gilsland Nthumb .......42  E5
Gilwern Mons ..........21  G8
Girton Cambs ..........16  C2
Girvan S Ayrs ..........40  C3
Gisburn Lancs ..........33  G2
Glamis Angus ..........51  J3
Glanton Nthumb .......47  K7
Glapwell Derbys .......30  B3
Glasbury Powys ........20  F6
Glasgow C Glas .........45  J2
Glaston Rutlnd .........23  J1
Glastonbury Somset ...12  F7
Glemsford Suffk ........17  G3
Glenbarr Ag & B .......44  A4
Glenborrodale Highld ..52  D5
Glencaple D & G ........41  K5
Glencoe Highld .........53  H5
Glendaruel Ag & B .....49  H5
Glendevon P & K .......50  E6
Glenelg Highld .........57  H7
Glenfarg P & K ..........51  G5
Glenfinnan Highld ......52  F3
Glenkindie Abers .......55  H3
Glenlivet Moray .........59  K6
Glenluce D & G ..........40  C5
Glen Maye IoM ..........36  b3
Glenridding Cumb ......37  G2
Glenrothes Fife .........51  H6
Glentham Lincs .........35  G7
Glossop Derbys .........33  J7
Gloucester Gloucs .....21  M7
Glyn Ceiriog Wrexhm ..27  K6
Glyncorrwg Neath .....19  L6
Glynde E Susx ..........10  C7
Glynneath Neath .......19  L5
Glyntawe Powys .......20  C8
Gnosall Staffs ..........28  F7
Goathland N York ......39  H3
Goathurst Somset ......12  D7
Gobowen Shrops .......27  L6
Godalming Surrey .......9  J2
Godmanchester
  Cambs ..................23  M4
Godshill IoW .............8  F7
Godstone Surrey .......10  C3
Goginan Cerdgn ........20  B3
Golborne Wigan .......32  F6
Goldhanger Essex ......17  G6
Golspie Highld ..........64  E7
Gomshall Surrey .........9  K2
Goodwick Pembks ......18  C3
Goole E R Yk ............34  E4
Goostrey Ches E ........28  E3
Gordon Border ..........47  G5
Gorebridge Mdloth ....46  D4
Gorey Jersey .............7  c1
Goring Oxon .............14  D5
Gorleston on Sea
  Norfk ...................25  L5
Gorran Haven Cnwll ....2  F6
Gorseinon Swans ......19  J6
Gosberton Lincs ........31  H6
Gosforth Cumb .........36  D3
Gosforth N u Ty ........43  J5

Gosport Hants ...........8  F5
Goudhurst Kent .........10  F4
Gourock Inver ..........49  K5
Gowerton Swans .......19  J6
Goxhill N Linc ..........35  H5
Grain Medway ..........11  G2
Grainthorpe Lincs ......35  K6
Grampound Cnwll .......2  F6
Grandes Rocques
  Guern ....................6  a1
Grange Cumb ...........36  F2
Grangemouth Falk .....50  E8
Grange-over-Sands
  Cumb ..................37  G5
Grantham Lincs ........30  F6
Grantown-on-Spey
  Highld ..................59  J6
Grantshouse Border ...47  H4
Grasmere Cumb ........37  G3
Grassington N York ....38  A6
Graveley Herts .........16  B4
Gravesend Kent ........10  E2
Grays Thurr .............10  E1
Great Ayton N York ...38  F3
Great Badminton
  S Glos ..................13  H3
Great Bardfield Essex ..16  E4
Great Barford Bed .....23  L5
Great Bircham Norfk ..24  E3
Great Blakenham
  Suffk ...................17  J3
Great Casterton
  Rutlnd ..................30  F8
Great Chesterford
  Essex ...................16  D3
Great Dalby Leics ......30  D7
Great Dunmow
  Essex ...................16  E5
Great Durnford Wilts ...8  E5
Great Gidding Cambs ..23  L3
Great Gransden
  Cambs ..................16  B2
Greatham Hants .........9  H3
Great Harwood
  Lancs ...................33  G4
Great Haywood
  Staffs ...................29  G7
Great Hockham
  Norfk ...................25  G6
Great Kimble Bucks ...14  F3
Great Langdale
  Cumb ..................36  F3
Great Malvern Worcs ..21  L5
Great Massingham
  Norfk ...................24  E4
Great Missenden
  Bucks ..................14  F4
Great Notley Essex ....16  F5
Great Ponton Lincs ....30  F6
Great Sampford
  Essex ...................16  E4
Great Saughall
  Ches W .................28  B3
Great Shefford
  W Berk .................14  B6
Great Shelford
  Cambs ..................16  C3
Great Smeaton
  N York ..................38  D3
Greatstone-on-Sea
  Kent ....................11  J6
Great Tew Oxon ........22  E7
Great Torrington
  Devon ....................4  E5
Great Wakering
  Essex ...................17  G8
Great Waltham
  Essex ...................16  E6
Great Witley Worcs ....21  L4
Great Yarmouth
  Norfk ...................25  L5
Great Yeldham Essex ..16  F4
Greenfield Flints .......27  K3
Green Hammerton
  N York ..................38  E7
Greenhead Nthumb ...42  E5
Greenhow Hill N York ..38  B6
Greenlaw Border .......47  G5
Greenloaning P & K ...50  D6
Greenock Inver ........49  L5
Greenodd Cumb ........36  F5
Greetham Rutlnd ......30  F7
Gresford Wrexhm ......27  L4
Greta Bridge Dur ......38  B3
Gretna D & G ...........42  B5
Gretna Green D & G ...42  B5
Greystoke Cumb .......42  C8
Grimsby NE Lin .........35  J5
Grimsthorpe Lincs .....31  G7
Grindleford Derbys ....29  J3
Gringley on the Hill
  Notts ...................34  E7

**Groby** Leics .................. 30 B8
**Grosmont** Mons ......... 21 H7
**Grouville** Jersey ........... 7 c2
**Grove** Oxon .............. 14 B5
**Guardbridge** Fife ...... 51 J5
**Guestling Green**
  E Susx ...................... 11 G6
**Guildford** Surrey ......... 9 K2
**Guisborough** R & Cl .. 38 F2
**Guiseley** Leeds ......... 33 K3
**Guist** Norfk ............... 25 G4
**Gullane** E Loth ......... 46 E2
**Gunness** N Linc ....... 34 E5
**Gunnislake** Cnwll ....... 3 K4
**Gunthorpe** Notts ...... 30 D5
**Gurnard** IoW ............... 8 E6
**Gussage All Saints**
  Dorset ........................ 8 A5
**Gutcher** Shet .............. 61 d2
**Guyhirn** Cambs ......... 24 B5
**Gweek** Cnwll ............... 2 D7
**Gwernymynydd**
  Flints ....................... 27 K4
**Gwithian** Cnwll ............ 2 C6
**Gwyddelwern**
  Denbgs ..................... 27 J5

## H

**Hackland** Ork ............. 65 b3
**Hackness** N York ...... 39 J4
**Hackney** Gt Lon ........ 15 K5
**Haddenham** Bucks .... 14 E3
**Haddenham** Cambs ... 24 C7
**Haddington** E Loth ... 46 F3
**Haddiscoe** Norfk ...... 25 L6
**Hadleigh** Essex ........ 16 F8
**Hadleigh** Suffk ......... 17 H3
**Hadlow** Kent ............. 10 E4
**Hagworthingham**
  Lincs ....................... 31 J3
**Hailsham** E Susx ...... 10 E7
**Halberton** Devon ......... 5 J6
**Hales** Norfk ............... 25 K6
**Halesowen** Dudley .... 22 A3
**Halesworth** Suffk ...... 25 K7
**Halifax** Calder .......... 33 K4
**Halkirk** Highld .......... 65 G2
**Halstead** Essex ........ 16 F4
**Halstead** Kent .......... 10 D3
**Haltwhistle** Nthumb .. 42 E5
**Halwell** Devon ............. 6 B6
**Halwill Junction**
  Devon ....................... 4 D7
**Hambledon** Hants ....... 9 G4
**Hamble-le-Rice**
  Hants ........................ 8 E5
**Hambleton** Lancs ...... 32 D3
**Hamilton** S Lans ....... 45 K3
**Hammersmith** Gt Lon .. 15 J6
**Hampstead Norreys**
  W Berk ..................... 14 C6
**Hampsthwaite**
  N York ..................... 38 C7
**Hamstreet** Kent ......... 11 H5
**Handcross** W Susx .... 10 B5
**Handley** Ches W ........ 28 C4
**Hanley** C Stke ........... 28 F5
**Happisburgh** Norfk .... 25 K3
**Harbertonford**
  Devon ....................... 6 B6
**Hardwicke** Gloucs ..... 13 H1
**Hare Street** Herts ..... 16 C4
**Harewood** Leeds ...... 33 L3
**Harewood End**
  Herefs ..................... 21 J7
**Harlech** Gwynd ......... 26 E6
**Harleston** Norfk ........ 25 J7
**Harlosh** Highld .......... 56 C5
**Harlow** Essex ............ 16 C6
**Harlyn** Cnwll ............... 2 E4
**Haroldswick** Shet ...... 61 d1
**Harpenden** Herts ...... 15 H3
**Harrogate** N York ..... 38 C7
**Harrold** Bed ............. 23 K5
**Harrow** Gt Lon ......... 15 H5
**Harston** Cambs ......... 16 C3
**Hartburn** Nthumb ..... 43 H3
**Hartest** Suffk ........... 17 G3
**Hartfield** E Susx ...... 10 D5
**Hartington** Derbys .... 29 H4
**Hartland** Devon .......... 4 C5
**Hartlepool** Hartpl ..... 43 M8
**Hartley Wintney**
  Hants ...................... 14 E7
**Hartpury** Gloucs ....... 21 L7
**Harvington** Worcs ..... 22 B5
**Harwich** Essex ......... 17 K4
**Haseley** Warwks ....... 22 D4
**Haslemere** Surrey ....... 9 J3

**Hassocks** W Susx ..... 10 B6
**Hastings** E Susx ....... 10 F7
**Hatch Beauchamp**
  Somset ................... 12 D8
**Hatfield** Donc ........... 34 D5
**Hatfield** Herts .......... 15 J3
**Hatfield Broad Oak**
  Essex ..................... 16 D5
**Hatfield Heath** Essex .. 16 D5
**Hatfield Peverel**
  Essex ..................... 16 F6
**Hatherleigh** Devon ...... 4 E6
**Hathern** Leics .......... 30 B7
**Hathersage** Derbys ... 29 J2
**Hatton** Abers ........... 61 H5
**Havant** Hants ............. 9 G5
**Havenstreet** IoW ......... 8 F6
**Haverfordwest**
  Pembks ................... 18 C5
**Haverhill** Suffk ......... 16 E3
**Hawarden** Flints ...... 27 L3
**Hawes** N York .......... 37 L4
**Hawick** Border ......... 46 F7
**Hawkedon** Suffk ....... 16 F3
**Hawkhurst** Kent ....... 10 F5
**Hawkinge** Kent ......... 11 K4
**Hawkshead** Cumb .... 37 G4
**Hawnby** N York ........ 38 E4
**Haworth** C Brad ....... 33 J3
**Haxby** C York ........... 38 F7
**Haxey** N Linc .......... 34 E6
**Haydon Bridge**
  Nthumb .................. 42 F5
**Hayle** Cnwll ............... 2 C6
**Hay-on-Wye** Powys .. 21 G6
**Haywards Heath**
  W Susx ................... 10 B6
**Hazel Grove** Stockp .. 28 F2
**Heacham** Norfk ....... 24 D3
**Headcorn** Kent ......... 11 G4
**Heanor** Derbys ........ 29 L5
**Heath** Derbys ........... 29 L3
**Heathfield** E Susx .... 10 E6
**Hebden Bridge**
  Calder .................... 33 J4
**Heckington** Lincs ..... 31 G5
**Hedge End** Hants ....... 8 E4
**Hednesford** Staffs .... 29 G8
**Hedon** E R Yk .......... 35 J5
**Helensburgh** Ag & B .. 49 L5
**Hellifield** N York ...... 37 L7
**Helmingham** Suffk ... 17 K2
**Helmsdale** Highld .... 65 G6
**Helmsley** N York ...... 38 F5
**Helpringham** Lincs ... 31 G5
**Helsby** Ches W ........ 28 C3
**Helston** Cnwll ............ 2 C7
**Hemel Hempstead**
  Herts ...................... 15 H3
**Hempnall** Norfk ....... 25 J6
**Hemsby** Norfk .......... 25 L4
**Hemsworth** Wakefd .. 34 B5
**Hemyock** Devon ......... 5 K6
**Hendy** Carmth .......... 19 J6
**Henfield** W Susx ......... 9 L4
**Henham** Essex ......... 16 D4
**Henley-in-Arden**
  Warwks ................... 22 C4
**Henley-on-Thames**
  Oxon ...................... 14 E5
**Henllan** Denbgs ....... 27 J3
**Henlow** C Beds ........ 23 L6
**Henstead** Suffk ........ 25 L7
**Henstridge** Somset ..... 7 K1
**Hereford** Herefs ...... 21 J6
**Hermitage** W Berk ... 14 C6
**Herne Bay** Kent ....... 11 J2
**Hersden** Kent .......... 11 K3
**Herstmonceux**
  E Susx .................... 10 E6
**Hertford** Herts ......... 15 K3
**Hessle** E R Yk .......... 35 G4
**Heswall** Wirral ......... 27 L2
**Hethersett** Norfk ..... 25 H5
**Heversham** Cumb .... 37 H5
**Hexham** Nthumb ...... 43 G5
**Hexworthy** Devon ....... 3 M4
**Heybrook Bay** Devon .. 3 K6
**Heysham** Lancs ....... 37 G7
**Heytesbury** Wilts ..... 13 J6
**Hibaldstow** N Linc ... 35 G6
**Hickstead** W Susx .... 10 B6
**Higham Ferrers**
  Nhants .................... 23 K4
**Highampton** Devon ..... 4 E6
**High Bentham**
  N York .................... 37 J6
**Highbridge** Somset ... 12 D6
**Highclere** Hants ...... 14 B7
**High Ercall** Wrekin ... 28 D7
**Higher Town** IoS ........ 2 b1
**High Halden** Kent .... 11 G5

**High Hesket** Cumb .... 42 C7
**Highley** Shrops ........ 21 L3
**High Roding** Essex ... 16 E5
**Highworth** Swindn ... 13 M3
**High Wycombe**
  Bucks ..................... 14 F4
**Hildenborough** Kent .. 10 D4
**Hill Brow** Hants .......... 9 H3
**Hill of Fearn** Highld .. 59 G2
**Hillswick** Shet .......... 61 b3
**Hilmarton** Wilts ....... 13 K4
**Hilton** Derbys .......... 29 J6
**Hinckley** Leics ......... 22 E2
**Hinderwell** N York ... 39 G2
**Hindhead** Surrey ........ 9 J3
**Hindon** Wilts ............ 13 J7
**Hingham** Norfk ........ 25 G5
**Hipswell** N York ....... 38 B4
**Hirwaun** Rhondd ...... 12 A2
**Histon** Cambs .......... 16 C2
**Hitcham** Suffk .......... 17 H3
**Hitchin** Herts ........... 23 M7
**Hockley** Essex .......... 17 G7
**Hockliffe** C Beds ...... 23 K7
**Hoddesdon** Herts ..... 15 K3
**Hodnet** Shrops ........ 28 D6
**Hogsthorpe** Lincs .... 31 L3
**Holbeach** Lincs ........ 31 J7
**Holbeton** Devon ......... 3 L5
**Holbrook** Suffk ........ 17 J4
**Holbury** Hants ........... 8 E5
**Holkham** Norfk ........ 24 F2
**Hollingbourne** Kent .. 11 G3
**Holmbury St Mary**
  Surrey ...................... 9 L2
**Holmes Chapel**
  Ches E ................... 28 E3
**Holme upon**
  **Spalding Moor**
  E R Yk .................... 34 E3
**Holmfirth** Kirk ......... 33 K6
**Holmrook** Cumb ...... 36 D4
**Holne** Devon .............. 6 A5
**Holsworthy** Devon ...... 4 C6
**Holt** Norfk ............... 25 H3
**Holt** Wilts ................ 13 J5
**Holt** Wrexhm ........... 28 B4
**Holt Heath** Worcs .... 21 L4
**Holton le Clay** Lincs .. 35 J6
**Holyhead** IoA .......... 26 B2
**Holy Island** Nthumb .. 47 L5
**Holytown** N Lans ..... 45 L2
**Holywell** Dorset ......... 7 J2
**Holywell** Flints ........ 27 K3
**Homersfield** Suffk .... 25 J7
**Honingham** Norfk .... 25 H5
**Honington** Suffk ...... 24 F7
**Honiton** Devon .......... 6 E2
**Hook** Hants ............. 14 E7
**Hoo St Werburgh**
  Medway .................. 10 F2
**Hope** Derbys ........... 29 J2
**Hope** Devon .............. 6 A7
**Hope** Flints ............. 27 L4
**Hope Bowdler**
  Shrops .................... 21 J2
**Hopeman** Moray ...... 59 K3
**Hope under**
  **Dinmore** Herefs ... 21 J5
**Hopton on Sea**
  Norfk ..................... 25 M5
**Horam** E Susx ......... 10 D6
**Horley** Surrey .......... 10 B4
**Hornby** Lancs .......... 37 J6
**Horncastle** Lincs ..... 31 H3
**Horndean** Hants ......... 9 G4
**Horns Cross** Devon ..... 4 D5
**Hornsea** E R Yk ....... 35 H3
**Horrabridge** Devon ..... 3 L4
**Horsey** Norfk ........... 25 L4
**Horsforth** Leeds ...... 33 L3
**Horsham** W Susx ....... 9 L3
**Horsley** Nthumb ...... 43 H5
**Horton** Dorset ........... 8 B5
**Horton** Somset .......... 6 F1
**Horton-cum-Studley**
  Oxon ..................... 14 D3
**Horton-in-**
  **Ribblesdale**
  N York .................... 37 L6
**Horwich** Bolton ....... 32 F5
**Hoton** Leics ............. 30 C7
**Houghton-le-Spring**
  Sundld ................... 43 K6
**Houghton on the**
  **Hill** Leics .............. 23 G1
**Hounslow** Gt Lon .... 15 H6
**Houton** Ork ............. 65 b4
**Hove** Br & H ............ 10 B7
**Hovingham** N York .. 38 F5
**Howden** E R Yk ....... 34 E4
**Hoxne** Suffk ............ 25 J7

**Hoylake** Wirral ........ 32 B7
**Hoyland Nether**
  Barns ..................... 34 B6
**Hucknall** Notts ........ 30 B5
**Huddersfield** Kirk .... 33 K5
**Hugh Town** IoS ......... 2 a2
**Hull, Kingston upon**
  C KuH .................... 35 G4
**Humberston** NE Lin .. 35 J6
**Humbie** E Loth ........ 46 E4
**Hume** Border .......... 47 G5
**Hungerford** W Berk .. 14 B6
**Hunmanby** N York ... 39 K5
**Hunstanton** Norfk ... 24 D2
**Huntingdon** Cambs .. 23 M3
**Huntley** Gloucs ....... 21 L7
**Huntly** Abers ........... 60 C5
**Hursley** Hants ........... 8 E4
**Hurstbourne Priors**
  Hants ...................... 8 E2
**Hurstbourne Tarrant**
  Hants ..................... 14 B7
**Hurst Green** E Susx .. 10 F5
**Hurst Green** Lancs ... 32 F3
**Hurstpierpoint**
  W Susx ................... 10 B6
**Hurworth-on-Tees**
  Darltn .................... 38 C3
**Husbands Bosworth**
  Leics ...................... 23 G2
**Husborne Crawley**
  C Beds .................. 23 K6
**Huttoft** Lincs .......... 31 L3
**Hutton-le-Hole**
  N York .................... 39 G4
**Hyde** Tamesd ......... 33 H7
**Hynish** Ag & B ........ 48 b3
**Hythe** Hants .............. 8 E5
**Hythe** Kent .............. 11 J5

## I

**Ibstock** Leics .......... 29 K8
**Ideford** Devon ........... 6 C4
**Ilchester** Somset ..... 12 F8
**Ilfracombe** Devon ....... 4 E3
**Ilkeston** Derbys ....... 29 L5
**Ilkley** C Brad .......... 33 K3
**Ilminster** Somset ....... 7 G1
**Immingham** NE Lin .. 35 H5
**Immingham Dock**
  NE Lin .................... 35 H5
**Inchnadamph** Highld .. 63 H5
**Ingatestone** Essex ... 16 E7
**Ingham** Lincs ........... 30 F2
**Ingleton** N York ....... 37 K6
**Ingoldmells** Lincs .... 31 L3
**Inkberrow** Worcs ..... 22 B5
**Innellan** Ag & B ....... 49 K6
**Innerleithen** Border .. 46 D6
**Insch** Abers ............. 60 D6
**Insh** Highld ............. 54 C4
**Instow** Devon ............. 4 D4
**Inverallochy** Abers ... 61 G3
**Inveran** Highld ........ 64 C7
**Inveraray** Ag & B ..... 49 J3
**Inverasdale** Highld ... 57 H2
**Inverbervie** Abers .... 55 L6
**Invergarry** Highld .... 53 K2
**Invergordon** Highld .. 58 F3
**Invergowrie** P & K ... 51 H4
**Inverinate** Highld ..... 57 J6
**Inverkeilor** Angus .... 51 L2
**Inverkeithing** Fife ... 46 B2
**Inverkeithny** Abers ... 60 D5
**Inverkip** Inver ......... 49 K6
**Invermoriston**
  Highld .................... 58 D7
**Inverness** Highld ..... 58 F5
**Inverurie** Abers ....... 55 L3
**Ipplepen** Devon ......... 6 B5
**Ipstones** Staffs ....... 29 G5
**Ipswich** Suffk ......... 17 J3
**Irchester** Nhants ..... 23 J4
**Ireby** Cumb ............ 42 A7
**Ironbridge** Wrekin ... 21 K1
**Irthlingborough**
  Nhants .................. 23 K3
**Irvine** N Ayrs .......... 45 G5
**Isle of Whithorn** D & G .. 40 F7
**Isleornsay** Highld .... 57 G7
**Islington** Gt Lon ...... 15 K5
**Itchen Abbas** Hants ... 8 F3
**Iver** Bucks .............. 15 G5
**Ivinghoe** Bucks ...... 15 G3
**Ivybridge** Devon ....... 3 M5
**Iwade** Kent ............. 11 G2
**Iwerne Minster**
  Dorset ..................... 7 L1
**Ixworth** Suffk .......... 25 G8

## J

Jarrow S Tyne 43 K5
Jedburgh Border 47 G7
Jerbourg Guern 6 b2
Jevington E Susx 10 D7
John o' Groats Highld 65 J1
Johnshaven Abers 55 L7
Johnston Pembks 18 C5
Johnstone Rens 49 M6
Jurby IoM 36 c1

## K

Kames Ag & B 49 H6
Keelby Lincs 35 H5
Kegworth Leics 30 B6
Keighley C Brad 33 J3
Keiss Highld 65 J2
Keith Moray 60 B4
Keld N York 37 L3
Kelham Notts 30 D4
Kelso Border 47 G6
Kelvedon Essex 17 G5
Kemble Gloucs 13 K2
Kemnay Abers 55 K3
Kempsey Worcs 21 M5
Kempston Bed 23 K3
Kendal Cumb 37 H4
Kenilworth Warwks 22 D3
Kenmore P & K 50 D3
Kennacraig Ag & B 49 G6
Kennford Devon 6 C3
Kenninghall Norfk 25 G7
Kentallen Highld 53 G5
Kentford Suffk 16 F2
Kenton Devon 6 C4
Kerry Powys 20 F2
Kessingland Suffk 25 L6
Keswick Cumb 36 F2
Kettering Nhants 23 J3
Kettlewell N York 37 M6
Ketton Rutlnd 23 K1
Keymer W Susx 10 B6
Keynsham BaNES 13 G4
Keyston Cambs 23 K3
Keyworth Notts 30 C6
Kibworth Beauchamp Leics 23 G2
Kidderminster Worcs 21 M3
Kidlington Oxon 14 C3
Kidsgrove Staffs 28 F4
Kidwelly Carmth 19 G5
Kielder Nthumb 42 D3
Kilberry Ag & B 48 F6
Kilbirnie N Ayrs 45 G3
Kilburn Derbys 29 K5
Kilburn N York 38 E5
Kilchattan Ag & B 44 E3
Kilchoan Highld 52 C4
Kilchrenan Ag & B 49 J2
Kilcreggan Ag & B 49 K5
Kildale N York 38 F3
Kildrummy Abers 55 H3
Kildwick N York 33 J3
Kilfinan Ag & B 49 H5
Kilgetty Pembks 18 E5
Kilham E R Yk 39 K6
Kilkenzie Ag & B 44 B5
Kilkhampton Cnwll 4 C6
Killearn Stirlg 50 B7
Killiecrankie P & K 54 D7
Killin Stirlg 50 B4
Kilmacolm Inver 49 L6
Kilmany Fife 51 J5
Kilmarnock E Ayrs 45 H4
Kilmartin Ag & B 49 G4
Kilmaurs E Ayrs 45 H4
Kilmelford Ag & B 49 G3
Kilmorack Highld 58 D5
Kilninver Ag & B 49 G2
Kilsyth N Lans 50 C8
Kilve Somset 5 K3
Kilwinning N Ayrs 45 G4
Kimberley Norfk 25 H5
Kimbolton Cambs 23 L4
Kinbrace Highld 64 E5
Kincardine Fife 50 E7
Kincardine O'Neil Abers 55 J4
Kincraig Highld 54 C4
Kineton Warwks 22 E5
Kingsbarns Fife 51 K5
Kingsbridge Devon 6 B7
Kingsbury Warwks 22 D2
Kingsclere Hants 14 C7
King's Cliffe Nhants 23 K1
Kingsdown Kent 11 L4

Kingsfold W Susx 9 L3
Kingskerswell Devon 6 C5
Kingsland Herefs 21 H4
Kings Langley Herts 15 H4
Kingsley Staffs 29 G5
King's Lynn Norfk 24 D4
King's Mills Guern 6 a2
Kingsnorth Kent 11 H4
King's Somborne Hants 8 D3
King's Stag Dorset 7 K2
King's Stanley Gloucs 13 H2
Kingsteignton Devon 6 C4
Kingstone Herefs 21 H6
Kingston on Spey Moray 59 L3
Kingston upon Hull C KuH 35 G4
Kingston upon Thames Gt Lon 15 J6
Kingswear Devon 6 C6
Kings Worthy Hants 8 E3
Kington Herefs 21 G5
Kingussie Highld 54 B4
Kinlochbervie Highld 63 H3
Kinlocheil Highld 53 G3
Kinlochewe Highld 57 J3
Kinlochleven Highld 53 J5
Kinloch Rannoch P & K 50 C2
Kinloss Moray 59 J3
Kinmel Bay Conwy 27 H2
Kinneff Abers 55 L6
Kinross P & K 50 F6
Kintbury W Berk 14 B6
Kintore Abers 55 L3
Kippen Stirlg 50 C7
Kirby Misperton N York 39 G5
Kirby Muxloe Leics 22 F1
Kirkabister Shet 61 c6
Kirkbean D & G 41 K6
Kirkbride Cumb 42 A6
Kirkburton Kirk 33 K5
Kirkby Knows 32 D6
Kirkby-in-Ashfield Notts 30 B4
Kirkby Lonsdale Cumb 37 J5
Kirkby Malzeard N York 38 C5
Kirkbymoorside N York 39 G5
Kirkby Stephen Cumb 37 K3
Kirkcaldy Fife 51 H7
Kirkcolm D & G 40 B5
Kirkconnel D & G 45 K6
Kirkcowan D & G 40 D5
Kirkcudbright D & G 41 G6
Kirkham Lancs 32 D4
Kirkhill Highld 58 E5
Kirkinner D & G 40 E6
Kirkintilloch E Duns 45 K1
Kirk Langley Derbys 29 K6
Kirk Michael IoM 36 b2
Kirkmichael P & K 50 F2
Kirkmichael S Ayrs 45 G6
Kirknewton Nthumb 47 J6
Kirkoswald Cumb 42 D7
Kirkoswald S Ayrs 44 F6
Kirkpatrick-Fleming D & G 42 B5
Kirkwall Ork 65 c4
Kirkwhelpington Nthumb 43 H4
Kirriemuir Angus 51 J2
Kirtlington Oxon 31 J6
Kirton in Lindsey N Linc 34 F6
Kislingbury Nhants 23 H4
Knaphill Surrey 15 G7
Knaresborough N York 38 D7
Knarsdale Nthumb 42 E6
Knebworth Herts 15 J2
Knighton Powys 21 G3
Knightwick Worcs 21 L5
Knockan Highld 63 H6
Knockin Shrops 27 L7
Knottingley Wakefd 34 C4
Knowl Hill W & M 14 F5
Knutsford Ches E 28 E3
Kyleakin Highld 57 G6
Kyle of Lochalsh Highld 57 G6
Kylerhea Highld 57 G7

## L

Laceby NE Lin 35 H6
Ladock Cnwll 2 E5
Ladybank Fife 51 H5
Laggan Highld 54 A5
La Grève de Lecq Jersey 7 a1
Laide Highld 62 E8
Lairg Highld 64 C6
Lakenheath Suffk 24 E7
Lamberhurst Kent 10 E5
Lambourn W Berk 14 B6
Lamerton Devon 3 K3
Lamington S Lans 46 A4
Lamlash N Ayrs 44 D5
Lampeter Cerdgn 19 J2
Lamport Nhants 23 H3
Lanark S Lans 45 M4
Lancaster Lancs 37 H6
Lanchester Dur 43 J6
Lancing W Susx 9 L5
L'Ancresse Guern 6 b1
Landrake Cnwll 3 J5
Langham Rutlnd 30 E8
Langholm D & G 42 B4
Langport Somset 12 E8
Langthwaite N York 38 A3
Langtoft E R Yk 39 J6
Langton Matravers Dorset 8 A7
Langwathby Cumb 42 D7
Langworth Lincs 31 G3
Lanivet Cnwll 3 G4
Lapford Devon 5 G6
Largoward Fife 51 J6
Largs N Ayrs 44 F2
Larkhall S Lans 45 L3
Larkhill Wilts 8 B2
Lastingham N York 39 G4
Latchingdon Essex 17 G7
Latheron Highld 65 H4
Lauder Border 46 F5
Laugharne Carmth 18 F5
Launceston Cnwll 3 J3
Laurencekirk Abers 55 K6
Laurieston D & G 41 G5
Lavenham Suffk 17 G3
Lawers P & K 50 C3
Laxey IoM 36 c3
Laxfield Suffk 25 K8
Lazonby Cumb 42 D7
Leadenham Lincs 30 F5
Leaden Roding Essex 16 E6
Leadgate Dur 43 J6
Leadhills S Lans 45 M6
Leamington Spa Warwks 22 D4
Leatherhead Surrey 15 J7
Lechlade on Thames Gloucs 13 M2
Ledbury Herefs 21 L6
Lee Devon 4 E3
Leebotwood Shrops 21 J1
Leeds Leeds 33 L4
Leek Staffs 29 G4
Leeming Bar N York 38 C4
Lee-on-the-Solent Hants 8 F5
Legbourne Lincs 31 J2
Leicester C Leic 23 G1
Leigh Kent 10 D4
Leigh Wigan 32 F6
Leigh Sinton Worcs 21 L5
Leighton Buzzard C Beds 23 J7
Leintwardine Herefs 21 H3
Leiston Suffk 17 M2
Lelant Cnwll 2 C6
Lendalfoot S Ayrs 40 C3
Lenham Kent 11 G3
Lennoxtown E Duns 50 B8
Leominster Herefs 21 J4
L'Erée Guern 6 a2
Lerwick Shet 61 c6
Leslie Abers 60 D6
Leslie Fife 51 H6
Lesmahagow S Lans 45 L4
Leswalt D & G 40 B5
L'Etacq Jersey 7 a1
Letchworth Garden City Herts 16 B4
Letham Angus 51 K3
Letterston Pembks 18 C4
Leuchars Fife 51 J5
Leven E R Yk 35 H3
Leven Fife 51 J6
Levens Cumb 37 H5
Leverburgh W Isls 62 e7
Lewes E Susx 10 C7
Lewisham Gt Lon 10 C2

Leyburn N York 38 B4
Leyland Lancs 32 E5
Leysdown-on-Sea Kent 11 H2
Lhanbryde Moray 59 L3
Libberton S Lans 46 A5
Lichfield Staffs 29 H8
Lidgate Suffk 16 F2
Lifton Devon 3 J3
Lightwater Surrey 15 G7
Lilliesleaf Border 46 F7
Limpley Stoke Wilts 13 H5
Lincoln Lincs 30 F3
Lindale Cumb 37 G5
Lingfield Surrey 10 C4
Linlithgow W Loth 46 A3
Linton Cambs 16 D3
Linton Kent 10 F4
Liphook Hants 9 H3
Liskeard Cnwll 3 H4
Liss Hants 9 H3
Lissington Lincs 31 G2
Litcham Norfk 24 F4
Litchfield Hants 14 C7
Little Abington Cambs 16 D3
Little Berkhamsted Herts 15 K3
Littleborough Rochdl 33 H5
Little Brickhill M Keyn 23 J6
Little Bytham Lincs 30 F7
Little Clacton Essex 17 J5
Little Gaddesden Herts 15 G3
Littlehampton W Susx 9 K5
Littleport Cambs 24 D6
Littlestone-on-Sea Kent 11 J5
Little Stretton Shrops 21 H2
Little Torrington Devon 4 E5
Little Walsingham Norfk 25 G3
Liverpool Lpool 32 C7
Livingston W Loth 46 B3
Lizard Cnwll 2 D8
Llanaelhaearn Gwynd 26 C5
Llanarmon Dyffryn Ceiriog Wrexhm 27 K6
Llanarthne Carmth 19 H4
Llanbedr Gwynd 26 E6
Llanbedr-Dyffryn-Clwyd Denbgs 27 K4
Llanbedrog Gwynd 26 C6
Llanberis Gwynd 26 E4
Llanbister Powys 20 F3
Llanbrynmair Powys 20 D1
Llanddarog Carmth 19 H5
Llandderfel Gwynd 27 H6
Llanddulas Conwy 27 H3
Llandeilo Carmth 19 J4
Llandinam Powys 20 E2
Llandissilio Pembks 18 E4
Llandovery Carmth 19 K3
Llandre Cerdgn 20 B2
Llandrillo Denbgs 27 J6
Llandrindod Wells Powys 20 E4
Llandrinio Powys 27 L7
Llandudno Conwy 27 G2
Llandwrog Gwynd 26 D4
Llandybie Carmth 19 J5
Llandysul Cerdgn 19 G3
Llanelli Carmth 19 H6
Llanerchymedd IoA 26 D2
Llanerfyl Powys 27 J8
Llanfachraeth IoA 26 C2
Llanfair Caereinion Powys 27 J8
Llanfair Dyffryn Clwyd Denbgs 27 J4
Llanfairfechan Conwy 26 F3
Llanfairpwllgwyngyll IoA 26 D3
Llanfair Talhaiarn Conwy 27 H3
Llanfair Waterdine Shrops 21 G3
Llanfarian Cerdgn 20 A3
Llanfyllin Powys 27 K7
Llangadfan Powys 27 H8
Llangadog Carmth 19 K4
Llangammarch Wells Powys 20 D5
Llangedwyn Powys 27 K7
Llangefni IoA 26 D3
Llangeinor Brdgnd 19 L7
Llangeler Carmth 19 G3
Llangennith Swans 19 G6

| Place | County | Page | Grid |
|---|---|---|---|
| Llangernyw | Conwy | 27 | G3 |
| Llangoed | IoA | 26 | E2 |
| Llangollen | Denbgs | 27 | K5 |
| Llangors | Powys | 20 | F7 |
| Llangrannog | Cerdgn | 18 | F2 |
| Llangurig | Powys | 20 | D3 |
| Llangynidr | Powys | 20 | F7 |
| Llangynog | Powys | 27 | J7 |
| Llanhamlach | Powys | 20 | E7 |
| Llanharan | Rhondd | 12 | B3 |
| Llanidloes | Powys | 20 | D2 |
| Llanilar | Cerdgn | 20 | B3 |
| Llanllechid | Gwynd | 26 | E3 |
| Llannefydd | Conwy | 27 | H3 |
| Llanrhaeadr-ym-Mochnant | Powys | 27 | J7 |
| Llanrhidian | Swans | 19 | H6 |
| Llanrhystud | Cerdgn | 20 | A4 |
| Llanrug | Gwynd | 26 | E4 |
| Llanrwst | Conwy | 27 | G4 |
| Llansanffraid Glan Conwy | Conwy | 27 | G3 |
| Llansannan | Conwy | 27 | H3 |
| Llansantffraid | Cerdgn | 19 | H1 |
| Llansantffraid-ym-Mechain | Powys | 27 | K7 |
| Llansawel | Carmth | 19 | J3 |
| Llansteffan | Carmth | 19 | G5 |
| Llanthony | Mons | 21 | G7 |
| Llantrisant | Rhondd | 12 | B3 |
| Llantwit Major | V Glam | 5 | J1 |
| Llanuwchllyn | Gwynd | 27 | G6 |
| Llanvetherine | Mons | 21 | H8 |
| Llanvihangel Crucorney | Mons | 21 | G7 |
| Llanwddyn | Powys | 27 | J7 |
| Llanwnda | Gwynd | 26 | D4 |
| Llanwrda | Carmth | 19 | K3 |
| Llanwrtyd Wells | Powys | 20 | D5 |
| Llanybydder | Carmth | 19 | H2 |
| Llanymynech | Powys | 27 | L7 |
| Llanystumdwy | Gwynd | 26 | D6 |
| Llay | Wrexhm | 27 | L4 |
| Llechryd | Cerdgn | 18 | F3 |
| Llwyngwril | Gwynd | 26 | E8 |
| Llwynmawr | Wrexhm | 27 | K6 |
| Llynclys | Shrops | 27 | L7 |
| Llyswen | Powys | 20 | F6 |
| Lochailort | Highld | 52 | E3 |
| Lochaline | Highld | 52 | D6 |
| Locharbriggs | D & G | 41 | K4 |
| Lochawe | Ag & B | 53 | H7 |
| Loch Baghasdail | W Isls | 62 | c12 |
| Lochboisdale | W Isls | 62 | c12 |
| Lochbuie | Ag & B | 52 | D7 |
| Lochcarron | Highld | 57 | H5 |
| Lochdonhead | Ag & B | 52 | E7 |
| Lochearnhead | Stirlg | 50 | B4 |
| Lochgair | Ag & B | 49 | H4 |
| Lochgilphead | Ag & B | 49 | G4 |
| Lochgoilhead | Ag & B | 49 | K3 |
| Lochinver | Highld | 63 | G5 |
| Lochmaben | D & G | 41 | L4 |
| Lochmaddy | W Isls | 62 | d8 |
| Loch nam Madadh | W Isls | 62 | d8 |
| Lochranza | N Ayrs | 44 | D3 |
| Lochwinnoch | Rens | 45 | G2 |
| Lockerbie | D & G | 41 | L4 |
| Lockton | N York | 39 | H4 |
| Loddon | Norfk | 25 | K6 |
| Lofthouse | N York | 38 | B6 |
| Loftus | R & Cl | 39 | G2 |
| London | Gt Lon | 15 | K5 |
| London Colney | Herts | 15 | J4 |
| Long Ashton | N Som | 12 | F4 |
| Long Bennington | Lincs | 30 | E5 |
| Long Buckby | Nhants | 23 | G4 |
| Longburton | Dorset | 7 | J1 |
| Long Compton | Warwks | 22 | D6 |
| Long Crendon | Bucks | 14 | E3 |
| Long Eaton | Derbys | 30 | B6 |
| Longford | Gloucs | 21 | M7 |
| Longformacus | Border | 47 | G4 |
| Longframlington | Nthumb | 43 | J2 |
| Longham | Dorset | 8 | B6 |
| Longhorsley | Nthumb | 43 | J3 |
| Longhoughton | Nthumb | 47 | M7 |
| Long Itchington | Warwks | 22 | E4 |
| Long Lawford | Warwks | 22 | F3 |
| Long Marston | N York | 34 | C2 |
| Long Melford | Suffk | 17 | G3 |
| Longniddry | E Loth | 46 | E3 |
| Longnor | Shrops | 21 | J1 |
| Longnor | Staffs | 29 | H4 |
| Long Preston | N York | 37 | L7 |
| Longridge | Lancs | 32 | F3 |
| Longridge | W Loth | 45 | M2 |
| Longside | Abers | 61 | G5 |
| Long Stratton | Norfk | 25 | J6 |
| Long Sutton | Lincs | 31 | K7 |
| Long Sutton | Somset | 12 | F8 |
| Longton | Lancs | 32 | D4 |
| Longtown | Cumb | 42 | B5 |
| Longville in the Dale | Shrops | 21 | J2 |
| Looe | Cnwll | 3 | H5 |
| Lossiemouth | Moray | 59 | K3 |
| Lostwithiel | Cnwll | 3 | G5 |
| Loughborough | Leics | 30 | B7 |
| Louth | Lincs | 31 | J2 |
| Lowdham | Notts | 30 | D5 |
| Lower Diabaig | Highld | 57 | H4 |
| Lower Dicker | E Susx | 10 | D6 |
| Lower Peover | Ches E | 28 | E3 |
| Lower Swell | Gloucs | 22 | C7 |
| Lowestoft | Suffk | 25 | M6 |
| Loweswater | Cumb | 36 | E2 |
| Lowick | Nhants | 23 | K3 |
| Lowick | Nthumb | 47 | K5 |
| Low Row | N York | 37 | M4 |
| Lubenham | Leics | 23 | H2 |
| Ludborough | Lincs | 35 | J7 |
| Ludgershall | Wilts | 8 | D2 |
| Ludham | Norfk | 25 | K4 |
| Ludlow | Shrops | 21 | J3 |
| Lugton | E Ayrs | 45 | H3 |
| Lugwardine | Herefs | 21 | J6 |
| Lumphanan | Abers | 55 | J4 |
| Lumsden | Abers | 55 | H3 |
| Lunan | Angus | 51 | L2 |
| Lupton | Cumb | 37 | H5 |
| Luss | Ag & B | 49 | L4 |
| Lusta | Highld | 56 | C4 |
| Luton | Luton | 15 | H2 |
| Lutterworth | Leics | 22 | F2 |
| Lybster | Highld | 65 | H4 |
| Lydbury North | Shrops | 21 | H2 |
| Lydd | Kent | 11 | H6 |
| Lydford | Devon | 3 | L3 |
| Lydford on Fosse | Somset | 12 | F7 |
| Lydham | Shrops | 21 | G2 |
| Lydney | Gloucs | 13 | G2 |
| Lyme Regis | Dorset | 7 | G3 |
| Lyminge | Kent | 11 | J4 |
| Lymington | Hants | 8 | D6 |
| Lymm | Warrtn | 28 | E2 |
| Lympne | Kent | 11 | J5 |
| Lyndhurst | Hants | 8 | D5 |
| Lyneham | Wilts | 13 | K4 |
| Lyness | Ork | 65 | b5 |
| Lyng | Somset | 12 | E7 |
| Lynmouth | Devon | 5 | G3 |
| Lynton | Devon | 4 | F3 |
| Lyonshall | Herefs | 21 | G5 |
| Lytham St Anne's | Lancs | 32 | C4 |
| Lythe | N York | 39 | H3 |

## M

| Place | County | Page | Grid |
|---|---|---|---|
| Mablethorpe | Lincs | 31 | K2 |
| Macclesfield | Ches E | 28 | F3 |
| Macduff | Abers | 60 | E3 |
| Machrihanish | Ag & B | 44 | A5 |
| Machynlleth | Powys | 20 | C1 |
| Macmerry | E Loth | 46 | E3 |
| Maentwrog | Gwynd | 26 | F5 |
| Maerdy | Rhondd | 12 | B2 |
| Maesteg | Brdgnd | 19 | L7 |
| Maghull | Sefton | 32 | D6 |
| Maiden Bradley | Wilts | 13 | H7 |
| Maidencombe | Torbay | 6 | E5 |
| Maidenhead | W & M | 14 | F5 |
| Maiden Newton | Dorset | 7 | J3 |
| Maidstone | Kent | 10 | F3 |
| Mainsriddle | D & G | 41 | K6 |
| Malborough | Devon | 6 | A7 |
| Maldon | Essex | 17 | G4 |
| Malham | N York | 37 | L6 |
| Mallaig | Highld | 52 | D2 |
| Mallwyd | Gwynd | 27 | G8 |
| Malmesbury | Wilts | 13 | J3 |
| Malpas | Ches W | 28 | C5 |
| Maltby | Rothm | 34 | C7 |
| Malton | N York | 39 | G6 |
| Malvern | Worcs | 21 | L5 |
| Malvern Wells | Worcs | 21 | L6 |
| Manaccan | Cnwll | 2 | D7 |
| Manchester | Manch | 33 | G6 |
| Manea | Cambs | 24 | C6 |
| Manningtree | Essex | 17 | J4 |
| Manorbier | Pembks | 18 | D6 |
| Mansfield | Notts | 30 | B4 |
| Marazanvose | Cnwll | 2 | E5 |
| Marazion | Cnwll | 2 | B7 |
| March | Cambs | 24 | B6 |
| Marchwiel | Wrexhm | 28 | B5 |
| Marden | Kent | 10 | F4 |
| Mareham le Fen | Lincs | 31 | J4 |
| Margaretting | Essex | 16 | E6 |
| Margate | Kent | 11 | L2 |
| Mark | Somset | 12 | E6 |
| Mark Cross | E Susx | 10 | E5 |
| Market Bosworth | Leics | 22 | E1 |
| Market Deeping | Lincs | 31 | G8 |
| Market Drayton | Shrops | 28 | D6 |
| Market Harborough | Leics | 23 | H2 |
| Market Lavington | Wilts | 13 | K6 |
| Market Rasen | Lincs | 35 | H7 |
| Market Warsop | Notts | 30 | C3 |
| Market Weighton | E R Yk | 34 | F3 |
| Markfield | Leics | 30 | B8 |
| Markham Moor | Notts | 30 | D3 |
| Marksbury | BaNES | 13 | G5 |
| Marks Tey | Essex | 17 | G5 |
| Marlborough | Wilts | 13 | M4 |
| Marloes | Pembks | 18 | B5 |
| Marlow | Bucks | 14 | F5 |
| Marnhull | Dorset | 7 | K1 |
| Marshfield | S Glos | 13 | H4 |
| Marsh Gibbon | Bucks | 14 | D2 |
| Marske-by-the-Sea | R & Cl | 38 | F2 |
| Martin | Lincs | 31 | G4 |
| Martinstown | Dorset | 7 | J3 |
| Martlesham Heath | Suffk | 17 | K3 |
| Martock | Somset | 7 | H1 |
| Marton | Warwks | 22 | E4 |
| Marykirk | Abers | 55 | K7 |
| Maryport | Cumb | 41 | K7 |
| Mary Tavy | Devon | 3 | L3 |
| Marywell | Abers | 55 | J5 |
| Masham | N York | 38 | C5 |
| Matfield | Kent | 10 | E4 |
| Matlock | Derbys | 29 | K4 |
| Mattingley | Hants | 14 | E7 |
| Mauchline | E Ayrs | 45 | H5 |
| Maud | Abers | 60 | F4 |
| Maughold | IoM | 36 | d2 |
| Maulden | C Beds | 23 | K6 |
| Mawgan Porth | Cnwll | 2 | E4 |
| Mawnan Smith | Cnwll | 2 | D7 |
| Maybole | S Ayrs | 45 | G6 |
| Mayfield | E Susx | 10 | E5 |
| Mayfield | Staffs | 29 | H5 |
| Meare | Somset | 12 | F6 |
| Measham | Leics | 29 | K8 |
| Medstead | Hants | 9 | G3 |
| Meeth | Devon | 4 | E6 |
| Meifod | Powys | 27 | K8 |
| Meigle | P & K | 51 | H3 |
| Melbourn | Cambs | 16 | C3 |
| Melbourne | Derbys | 29 | K7 |
| Meliden | Denbgs | 27 | J2 |
| Melksham | Wilts | 13 | J5 |
| Melling | Lancs | 37 | J6 |
| Melmerby | Cumb | 42 | D7 |
| Melrose | Border | 46 | F6 |
| Meltham | Kirk | 33 | K5 |
| Melton Constable | Norfk | 25 | H3 |
| Melton Mowbray | Leics | 30 | D7 |
| Melvaig | Highld | 57 | G2 |
| Melvich | Highld | 64 | E2 |
| Memsie | Abers | 61 | G3 |
| Memus | Angus | 51 | J2 |
| Menai Bridge | IoA | 26 | E3 |
| Mentmore | Bucks | 14 | F3 |
| Meopham | Kent | 10 | E2 |
| Mere | Wilts | 13 | H7 |
| Meriden | Solhll | 22 | D3 |
| Merthyr Tydfil | Myr Td | 12 | B2 |
| Merton | Devon | 4 | E6 |
| Messingham | N Linc | 34 | E6 |
| Metfield | Suffk | 25 | K7 |
| Methil | Fife | 51 | J6 |
| Methlick | Abers | 60 | F5 |
| Methven | P & K | 50 | F4 |
| Methwold | Norfk | 24 | E6 |
| Mevagissey | Cnwll | 2 | F6 |
| Mexborough | Donc | 34 | B6 |
| Miabhig | W Isls | 62 | f3 |
| Miavaig | W Isls | 62 | f3 |
| Micheldever | Hants | 8 | F2 |
| Mickleton | Dur | 37 | M2 |
| Mickleton | Gloucs | 22 | C6 |
| Midbea | Ork | 65 | c2 |
| Middleham | N York | 38 | B4 |
| Middle Rasen | Lincs | 35 | G7 |
| Middlesbrough | Middsb | 38 | E2 |
| Middleton Cheney | Nhants | 22 | F6 |
| Middleton-in-Teesdale | Dur | 37 | M2 |
| Middleton-on-Sea | W Susx | 9 | J5 |
| Middleton on the Wolds | E R Yk | 34 | F2 |
| Middleton Stoney | Oxon | 14 | C2 |
| Middle Town | IoS | 2 | a2 |
| Middle Wallop | Hants | 8 | D3 |
| Middlewich | Ches E | 28 | E3 |
| Middlezoy | Somset | 12 | E7 |
| Midhurst | W Susx | 9 | J4 |
| Midsomer Norton | BaNES | 13 | G6 |
| Mid Yell | Shet | 61 | d2 |
| Milborne Port | Somset | 7 | J1 |
| Mildenhall | Suffk | 24 | E7 |
| Milfield | Nthumb | 47 | J6 |
| Milford | Surrey | 9 | J2 |
| Milford Haven | Pembks | 18 | C5 |
| Milford on Sea | Hants | 8 | D6 |
| Millbrook | Cnwll | 3 | K5 |
| Millbrook | Jersey | 7 | b2 |
| Millom | Cumb | 36 | E5 |
| Millport | N Ayrs | 44 | F3 |
| Milnathort | P & K | 50 | F6 |
| Milngavie | E Duns | 45 | J1 |
| Milton Abbas | Dorset | 7 | K2 |
| Milton Abbot | Devon | 3 | K3 |
| Milton Damerel | Devon | 4 | D6 |
| Milton Ernest | Bed | 23 | K5 |
| Milton Keynes | M Keyn | 23 | J6 |
| Milverton | Somset | 5 | K5 |
| Minchinhampton | Gloucs | 13 | J2 |
| Minehead | Somset | 5 | J3 |
| Minster | Kent | 11 | H2 |
| Minster | Kent | 11 | L2 |
| Minsterley | Shrops | 28 | B8 |
| Minster Lovell | Oxon | 14 | A3 |
| Mintlaw | Abers | 61 | G4 |
| Mirfield | Kirk | 33 | K5 |
| Misterton | Notts | 34 | E7 |
| Misterton | Somset | 7 | H2 |
| Mitcheldean | Gloucs | 21 | K7 |
| Mobberley | Ches E | 28 | E2 |
| Mochrum | D & G | 40 | E6 |
| Modbury | Devon | 3 | M5 |
| Moffat | D & G | 41 | L2 |
| Mold | Flints | 27 | K4 |
| Moniaive | D & G | 41 | H3 |
| Monifieth | Angus | 51 | K4 |
| Monkleigh | Devon | 4 | D5 |
| Monkton | S Ayrs | 45 | G5 |
| Monmouth | Mons | 21 | J8 |
| Montacute | Somset | 7 | H1 |
| Montford Bridge | Shrops | 28 | B7 |
| Montgomery | Powys | 20 | F1 |
| Montrose | Angus | 51 | L2 |
| Mont Saint | Guern | 6 | a2 |
| Monyash | Derbys | 29 | H3 |
| Monymusk | Abers | 55 | K3 |
| Morchard Bishop | Devon | 5 | G6 |
| Morcott | Rutlnd | 23 | J1 |
| Mordiford | Herefs | 21 | J6 |
| Morebattle | Border | 47 | H7 |
| Morecambe | Lancs | 37 | G6 |
| Moreton | Dorset | 7 | K3 |
| Moretonhampstead | Devon | 6 | B3 |
| Moreton-in-Marsh | Gloucs | 22 | C6 |
| Morfa Nefyn | Gwynd | 26 | B5 |
| Morley | Leeds | 33 | L4 |
| Morpeth | Nthumb | 43 | J3 |
| Morston | Norfk | 25 | G2 |
| Mortehoe | Devon | 4 | D3 |
| Mortimer | W Berk | 14 | D7 |
| Morville | Shrops | 21 | K2 |

Morwenstow Cnwll .........4 B5
Mossat Abers ................55 H3
Mosstodloch Moray ......59 L4
Mosterton Dorset ...........7 H2
Mostyn Flints ................27 K2
Motherby Cumb............37 G1
Motherwell N Lans........45 K3
Moulsford Oxon ...........14 D5
Moulton Nhants ...........23 H4
Mountain Ash
Rhondd.....................12 B2
Mountsorrel Leics ........30 C7
Mousehole Cnwll............2 B7
Moy Highld ..................58 F5
Muchalls Abers ............55 M5
Much Birch Herefs ........21 J7
Much Hadham Herts ....16 C5
Much Marcle Herefs......21 K6
Much Wenlock
Shrops .....................21 K1
Muddiford Devon............4 E4
Muirdrum Angus...........51 K3
Muirhead Angus...........51 H4
Muirkirk E Ayrs ............45 K5
Muir of Ord Highld .......58 D4
Muker N York ...............37 L4
Mullion Cnwll .................2 D8
Mundesley Norfk ..........25 K3
Mundford Norfk ...........24 E6
Mungrisdale Cumb.......42 B8
Munlochy Highld...........58 E4
Munslow Shrops ...........21 J2
Musselburgh E Loth......46 D3
Muthill P & K ...............50 D5

**N**

Nacton Suffk .................17 K4
Nailsea N Som ..............12 F4
Nailsworth Gloucs.........13 J2
Nairn Highld ................59 G4
Nantgaredig Carmth .....19 H4
Nantwich Ches E...........28 D5
Narberth Pembks ..........18 E5
Narborough Norfk.........24 E4
Naseby Nhants .............23 G3
Navenby Lincs ..............30 F4
Nayland Suffk ..............17 H4
Nazeing Essex ..............16 C6
Neath Neath..................19 K6
Necton Norfk ...............24 F5
Needham Market
Suffk ........................17 J2
Nefyn Gwynd ...............26 C5
Nelson Lancs ................33 H3
Nesscliffe Shrops..........28 B7
Neston Ches W .............27 L3
Nether Stowey
Somset .....................12 C7
Nether Wasdale Cumb...36 E3
Nethy Bridge Highld......54 D3
Nettlebed Oxon ............14 E5
Nevern Pembks .............18 E3
New Abbey D & G .........41 K5
New Aberdour Abers......60 F3
New Alresford Hants .......8 F3
Newark-on-Trent
Notts.........................30 E4
Newarthill N Lans.........45 L2
Newbiggin Dur ..............37 L1
Newbiggin N York ........38 A5
Newbiggin-by-the-
Sea Nthumb ..............43 K3
Newbigging S Lans........46 A5
Newbold on Stour
Warwks......................22 D5
New Bolingbroke
Lincs ........................31 J4
Newborough IoA ..........26 D4
Newbridge Caerph.........12 C2
Newbridge D & G .........41 K4
Newbridge-on-Wye
Powys ......................20 E4
New Buckenham
Norfk ........................25 H6
Newburgh Abers...........61 G6
Newburgh Fife...............51 G5
Newbury W Berk ...........14 C6
Newby Bridge Cumb.....37 G5
Newcastle Emlyn
Carmth .....................18 F3
Newcastleton Border.....42 C3
Newcastle-under-
Lyme Staffs ...............28 F7
Newcastle upon
Tyne N u Ty ...............43 K5
New Cumnock E Ayrs ....45 J6
New Deer Abers ............60 F5
Newent Gloucs .............21 L7
Newgale Pembks ..........18 C4

New Galloway D & G.....41 G4
New Grimsby IoS............2 a1
Newhaven E Susx..........10 C7
New Holland N Linc .....35 G4
Newick E Susx...............10 C6
New Luce D & G ..........40 C5
Newlyn Cnwll .................2 B7
Newmains N Lans.........45 L3
Newmarket Suffk..........16 E2
Newmill Moray..............60 B4
New Milton Hants ..........8 C6
Newnham Worcs...........21 K4
Newnham on
Severn Gloucs ..........13 G1
New Pitsligo Abers .......60 F4
Newport Essex ..............16 D4
Newport IoW ..................8 E6
Newport Newpt ............12 D3
Newport Pembks ..........18 D3
Newport Wrekin ...........28 E7
Newport-on-Tay Fife ....51 J4
Newport Pagnell
M Keyn......................23 J6
New Quay Cerdgn ........19 G1
Newquay Cnwll ..............2 E5
New Radnor Powys .......20 F4
New Romney Kent.........11 H5
Newsham N York ..........38 B3
Newton Abbot
Devon ........................6 C5
Newton Aycliffe Dur ....38 C2
Newton Ferrers
Devon ........................3 L6
Newton Ferry W Isls ....62 d8
Newtongrange
Mdloth ......................46 D4
Newtonhill Abers ..........55 M5
Newton Mearns
E Rens.......................45 J3
Newtonmore Highld......54 B4
Newton-on-the-
Moor Nthumb ...........43 J2
Newton on Trent
Lincs ........................30 E3
Newton St Cyres
Devon ........................6 C3
Newton Solney
Derbys ......................29 J7
Newton Stewart
D & G .......................40 E5
Newtown Herefs ...........21 K5
Newtown Powys ...........20 F2
New Tredegar
Caerph......................12 C2
Newtyle Angus..............51 H3
Neyland Pembks ...........18 D5
Nigg Highld .................59 G3
Ninfield E Susx.............10 E6
Niton IoW .....................8 F7
Nocton Lincs ................31 G4
Norham Nthumb...........47 J5
Normanton Wakefd ......34 B4
Northall Bucks ..............15 G2
Northallerton N York ....38 D4
Northam Devon ..............4 D4
Northampton
Nhants .....................23 H4
North Berwick E Loth....46 F2
North Cave E R Yk ........34 F4
Northchapel W Susx ......9 J3
North Chideock
Dorset ........................7 G3
North Cotes Lincs .........35 K6
North Creake Norfk ......24 F3
North Curry Somset......12 D8
North Dalton E R Yk......34 F2
North Elmham Norfk.....25 G4
North Ferriby E R Yk.....35 G4
Northfleet Kent.............10 E2
North Frodingham
E R Yk ......................35 H2
North Grimston
N York ......................39 H6
North Hayling Hants......9 G5
North Hykeham
Lincs ........................30 F3
Northiam E Susx ..........11 G6
North Kessock
Highld .......................58 F4
North Kilworth Leics ....23 G3
North Kyme Lincs .........31 H4
Northleach Gloucs ........22 C3
North Luffenham
RutInd .......................23 J1
North Molton Devon ......5 G4
North Muskham
Notts.........................30 E4
Northop Flints ..............27 K3
North Petherton
Somset .....................12 D7
North Rigton N York......33 L2
North Shields N Tyne ....43 K5

North Somercotes
Lincs ........................35 K6
North Walsham
Norfk ........................25 J3
North Waltham Hants.....8 F2
North Weald Bassett
Essex ........................16 D6
Northwich Ches W ........28 D3
North Wingfield
Derbys ......................29 K4
Northwold Norfk ..........24 E6
Norton-on-Derwent
N York ......................39 G6
Norton St Philip
Somset .....................13 H5
Norwich Norfk ..............25 J5
Nottingham C Nott .......30 C5
Nuneaton Warwks........22 E2
Nunney Somset.............13 H6
Nutley E Susx ...............10 C5

**O**

Oadby Leics .................23 G1
Oakham RutInd ............30 E8
Oakhill Somset.............13 G6
Oakley Bed...................23 K5
Oakley Bucks................14 D3
Oakley Hants................8 F2
Oare Wilts ...................13 L5
Oban Ag & B .................52 F7
Ochiltree E Ayrs ...........45 H5
Ockbrook Derbys ..........29 L6
Ockley Surrey .................9 L2
Odiham Hants ................9 G2
Offenham Worcs ...........22 B5
Ogbourne St George
Wilts .........................13 M4
Ogmore-by-Sea
V Glam ......................19 L8
Okehampton Devon........4 E7
Old Deer Abers..............61 G4
Old Grimsby IoS..............2 a1
Oldham Oldham............33 H6
Old Hurst Cambs ..........24 A7
Old Leake Lincs ............31 K5
Oldmeldrum Abers ........60 F6
Old Rayne Abers ...........60 D6
Old Sodbury S Glos.......13 H3
Old Stratford Nhants.....23 H6
Old Town IoS..................2 b2
Old Windsor W & M.......15 G6
Ollaberry Shet ..............61 b3
Ollerton Notts...............30 C3
Olney M Keyn ...............23 J5
Ombersley Worcs ..........21 M4
Onchan IoM .................36 C3
Onich Highld.................53 G5
Orford Suffk .................17 L3
Ormesby St
Margaret Norfk ........25 L4
Ormskirk Lancs .............32 D6
Orpington Gt Lon .........10 D2
Orsett Thurr .................10 E1
Orton Cumb .................37 J3
Osbournby Lincs ...........31 G6
Osmington Dorset ..........7 K4
Osmotherley N York .....38 E4
Ospringe Kent...............11 H3
Ossett Wakefd ..............33 L5
Oswaldkirk N York ........38 F5
Oswestry Shrops ...........27 L6
Otford Kent..................10 D3
Othery Somset..............12 E7
Otley Leeds...................33 K3
Otterbourne Hants .........8 E4
Otterburn Nthumb........43 G4
Otter Ferry Ag & B ........49 H5
Ottershaw Surrey...........9 K3
Otterton Devon ..............6 E4
Ottery St Mary
Devon ........................6 E3
Oundle Nhants .............23 K2
Outwell Norfk ..............24 C5
Overseal Derbys ...........29 K7
Overton Hants ...............8 F2
Overton Wrexhm ..........28 B5
Ower Hants ....................8 D4
Oxford Oxon ................14 C3
Oxted Surrey.................10 C3
Oxton Notts .................30 C5
Oxwich Swans ..............19 H7

**P**

Padbury Bucks ..............23 H7
Paddock Wood Kent......10 E4
Padiham Lancs .............33 G4

Padstow Cnwll................2 F4
Paignton Torbay.............6 C5
Pailton Warwks.............22 F3
Painswick Gloucs .........13 J1
Paisley Rens..................45 H2
Palnackie D & G ..........41 J6
Pandy Mons .................21 G7
Pangbourne W Berk .....14 D6
Pannal N York ..............33 L2
Pant-y-dwr Powys ........20 E3
Papworth Everard
Cambs ......................16 B2
Parracombe Devon .........4 F3
Pateley Bridge
N York ......................38 B6
Patna E Ayrs.................45 H6
Patrick IoM ...................36 b3
Patrington E R Yk..........35 J4
Patterdale Cumb...........37 G2
Pattishall Nhants...........23 H4
Paulton BaNES..............13 G5
Peacehaven E Susx........10 C7
Peasedown St John
BaNES .......................13 H5
Peasmarsh E Susx ........11 G6
Peebles Border..............46 C5
Peel IoM ......................36 b3
Pelynt Cnwll ...................3 H5
Pembrey Carmth...........19 G6
Pembridge Herefs .........21 H4
Pembroke Pembks ........18 D6
Pembroke Dock
Pembks......................18 D6
Pembury Kent...............10 E4
Penally Pembks.............18 E6
Penarth V Glam ............12 C4
Pencoed Brdgnd ...........12 A3
Pencraig Herefs.............21 J7
Pendine Carmth ...........18 F5
Pendock Worcs .............21 L6
Pendoggett Cnwll...........3 G3
Pengam Caerph.............12 C2
Penicuik Mdloth ...........46 C4
Penistone Barns ...........33 L6
Penkridge Staffs ...........29 G7
Penmachno Conwy .......27 G5
Penmaenmawr
Conwy ......................26 F3
Pennal Gwynd ..............20 B1
Pennan Abers ...............60 F3
Penpont D & G .............41 J3
Penrhyndeudraeth
Gwynd.......................26 E6
Penrith Cumb...............42 D8
Penryn Cnwll ..................2 E7
Pensford BaNES............13 G5
Penshurst Kent .............10 D4
Pensilva Cnwll.................3 J4
Pentewan Devon ............2 F6
Pentraeth IoA ...............26 D3
Pentrefoelas Conwy.......27 G5
Penybont Powys ...........20 F4
Pen-y-bont-fawr
Powys ......................27 J7
Penygroes Gwynd .........26 D4
Penzance Cnwll ..............2 B7
Perranporth Cnwll ..........2 D5
Pershore Worcs .............22 A5
Perth P & K ..................50 F4
Peterborough C Pete.....23 M1
Peterchurch Herefs .......21 H6
Peterculter C Aber.........55 L4
Peterhead Abers ...........61 H5
Peterlee Dur .................43 L7
Petersfield Hants ...........9 H4
Petton Devon ..................5 J5
Petworth W Susx ...........9 J4
Pevensey E Susx ...........10 E7
Pewsey Wilts.................13 L5
Pickering N York ...........39 G5
Piercebridge Darltn ......38 C2
Pierowall Ork................65 c1
Pillaton Cnwll.................3 J4
Pillerton Priors
Warwks......................22 D5
Pilling Lancs .................32 D3
Pinchbeck Lincs ...........31 H7
Pinwherry S Ayrs ..........40 C3
Pinxton Derbys .............29 L4
Pirbright Surrey.............15 G7
Pitcaple Abers ..............60 E6
Pitlochry P & K .............50 E2
Pitmedden Abers ..........60 F6
Pittenweem Fife............51 K6
Pleasley Derbys .............30 B4
Plockton Highld............57 H6
Pluckley Kent................11 G4
Plumpton E Susx ..........10 C6
Plumtree Notts .............30 C6
Plymouth C Plym ...........3 K5
Plympton C Plym ...........3 L5
Pocklington E R Yk........34 E2

| | | | |
|---|---|---|---|
| Polbathic Cnwll | 3 | J5 |
| Polegate E Susx | 10 | D7 |
| Polmont Falk | 50 | E8 |
| Polperro Cnwll | 3 | H5 |
| Polruan Cnwll | 3 | G5 |
| Polzeath Cnwll | 2 | F3 |
| Pontardawe Neath | 19 | K6 |
| Pontarddulais | | |
| Swans | 19 | J6 |
| Pontefract Wakefd | 34 | B5 |
| Ponteland Nthumb | 43 | J4 |
| Ponterwyd Cerdgn | 20 | C3 |
| Pontesbury Shrops | 28 | B8 |
| Pontlanfraith | | |
| Caerph | 12 | C2 |
| Pontrhydfendigaid | | |
| Cerdgn | 19 | K1 |
| Pontrilas Herefs | 21 | H7 |
| Pontyates Carmth | 19 | H5 |
| Pontyberem Carmth | 19 | H5 |
| Pontypool Torfn | 12 | D2 |
| Pontypridd Rhondd | 12 | B3 |
| Pool Leeds | 33 | L3 |
| Poole Poole | 8 | A6 |
| Poolewe Highld | 57 | H2 |
| Pooley Bridge Cumb | 37 | H3 |
| Porlock Somset | 5 | H3 |
| Porlock Weir Somset | 5 | H3 |
| Port Appin Ag & B | 52 | F6 |
| Port Askaig Ag & B | 48 | D6 |
| Portavadie Ag & B | 49 | H6 |
| Port Bannatyne | | |
| Ag & B | 49 | J6 |
| Port Carlisle Cumb | 42 | A5 |
| Port Charlotte | | |
| Ag & B | 48 | B7 |
| Portchester Hants | 8 | F5 |
| Port Ellen Ag & B | 48 | C8 |
| Port Erin IoM | 36 | a4 |
| Portesham Dorset | 7 | J3 |
| Port Eynon Swans | 19 | H7 |
| Port Glasgow Inver | 49 | L5 |
| Portgordon Moray | 60 | B3 |
| Porth Rhondd | 12 | B3 |
| Porthcawl Brdgnd | 19 | L8 |
| Porthcothan Cnwll | 2 | E4 |
| Porthcurno Cnwll | 2 | A8 |
| Port Henderson | | |
| Highld | 57 | G3 |
| Porthleven Cnwll | 2 | C7 |
| Porthmadog Gwynd | 26 | E6 |
| Porthtowan Cnwll | 2 | D6 |
| Portinscale Cumb | 36 | F2 |
| Port Isaac Cnwll | 2 | F3 |
| Portishead N Som | 12 | F4 |
| Portknockie Moray | 60 | C3 |
| Portlethen Abers | 55 | M5 |
| Portloe Cnwll | 2 | F6 |
| Port Logan D & G | 40 | C7 |
| Portmahomack | | |
| Highld | 59 | H2 |
| Portnacroish Ag & B | 53 | G6 |
| Portnahaven Ag & B | 48 | A7 |
| Port nan Long W Isls | 62 | d8 |
| Port Nis W Isls | 62 | i1 |
| Port of Menteith | | |
| Stirlg | 50 | B6 |
| Port of Ness W Isls | 62 | i1 |
| Portpatrick D & G | 40 | B6 |
| Portreath Cnwll | 2 | C6 |
| Portree Highld | 56 | E5 |
| Port St Mary IoM | 36 | a4 |
| Portscatho Cnwll | 2 | E7 |
| Portskerra Highld | 64 | D3 |
| Portslade-by-Sea | | |
| Br & H | 10 | B7 |
| Portsmouth C Port | 9 | G5 |
| Portsoy Abers | 60 | D3 |
| Port Talbot Neath | 19 | K7 |
| Port William D & G | 40 | E7 |
| Postbridge Devon | 3 | M3 |
| Postcombe Oxon | 14 | E4 |
| Potterne Wilts | 13 | K5 |
| Potters Bar Herts | 15 | J4 |
| Potton C Beds | 16 | B3 |
| Poulton-le-Fylde | | |
| Lancs | 32 | C3 |
| Powburn Nthumb | 47 | K7 |
| Powick Worcs | 21 | M5 |
| Poynton Ches E | 28 | F2 |
| Praa Sands Cnwll | 2 | C7 |
| Prees Shrops | 28 | C6 |
| Preesall Lancs | 32 | D3 |
| Prees Green Shrops | 28 | C6 |
| Prenteg Gwynd | 26 | E5 |
| Prestatyn Denbgs | 27 | J2 |
| Prestbury Ches E | 28 | F3 |
| Presteigne Powys | 21 | G4 |
| Preston Border | 41 | J4 |
| Preston Lancs | 32 | E4 |
| Preston Candover | | |
| Hants | 8 | F2 |

| | | | |
|---|---|---|---|
| Preston Capes | | |
| Nhants | 22 | F5 |
| Prestonpans E Loth | 46 | F3 |
| Prestwich Bury | 33 | G6 |
| Prestwick S Ayrs | 45 | G5 |
| Prestwood Bucks | 14 | F4 |
| Priddy Somset | 12 | F6 |
| Princes Risborough | | |
| Bucks | 14 | F4 |
| Princethorpe Warwks | 22 | E3 |
| Princetown Devon | 3 | L4 |
| Prospect Cumb | 41 | L7 |
| Prudhoe Nthumb | 43 | H5 |
| Pucklechurch S Glos | 13 | H4 |
| Puddletown Dorset | 7 | K3 |
| Pudsey Leeds | 33 | L4 |
| Pulborough W Susx | 9 | K4 |
| Pulford Ches W | 28 | B4 |
| Pulham St Mary | | |
| Norfk | 25 | J7 |
| Pumsaint Carmth | 19 | J3 |
| Purfleet Thurr | 10 | D1 |
| Purton Wilts | 13 | L3 |
| Pwll Carmth | 19 | H6 |
| Pwllheli Gwynd | 26 | C6 |
| Pyecombe W Susx | 10 | B6 |
| Pyle Brdgnd | 19 | L7 |

| | | | |
|---|---|---|---|
| **Q** | | |
| Quatt Shrops | 21 | L2 |
| Queensferry Flints | 27 | L3 |
| Quendon Essex | 16 | D4 |

| | | | |
|---|---|---|---|
| **R** | | |
| Rackenford Devon | 5 | H5 |
| Rackheath Norfk | 25 | J4 |
| Radcliffe on Trent | | |
| Notts | 30 | C6 |
| Radlett Herts | 15 | H4 |
| Radstock BaNES | 13 | G5 |
| Radwinter Essex | 16 | E4 |
| Radyr Cardif | 12 | C4 |
| Rafford Moray | 59 | J4 |
| Raglan Mons | 12 | E1 |
| Rainham Gt Lon | 10 | D1 |
| Rainham Medway | 10 | F2 |
| Rampside Cumb | 36 | F6 |
| Ramsbottom Bury | 33 | G5 |
| Ramsbury Wilts | 14 | A6 |
| Ramsey Cambs | 24 | A7 |
| Ramsey IoM | 36 | c2 |
| Ramsgate Kent | 11 | L2 |
| Rannoch Station | | |
| P & K | 53 | L5 |
| Rapness Ork | 65 | c2 |
| Rathen Abers | 61 | G3 |
| Rattray P & K | 51 | G3 |
| Raunds Nhants | 23 | K3 |
| Ravenglass Cumb | 36 | E4 |
| Ravenscar N York | 39 | J3 |
| Ravenstonedale | | |
| Cumb | 37 | K3 |
| Rawmarsh Rothm | 34 | B7 |
| Rawtenstall Lancs | 33 | G4 |
| Rayleigh Essex | 16 | F7 |
| Reading Readg | 14 | E6 |
| Reay Highld | 64 | F2 |
| Reculver Kent | 11 | K2 |
| Redbourn Herts | 15 | H3 |
| Redbrook Gloucs | 12 | F1 |
| Redbrook Wrexhm | 28 | C5 |
| Redcar R & Cl | 38 | F2 |
| Redditch Worcs | 22 | B4 |
| Redgrave Suffk | 25 | G7 |
| Redhill N Som | 12 | F5 |
| Redhill Surrey | 10 | B4 |
| Rednal Shrops | 28 | B6 |
| Red Roses Carmth | 18 | F5 |
| Red Row Nthumb | 43 | K2 |
| Redruth Cnwll | 2 | D6 |
| Red Wharf Bay IoA | 26 | D2 |
| Reedham Norfk | 25 | L5 |
| Reepham Norfk | 25 | H4 |
| Reigate Surrey | 10 | B4 |
| Reighton N York | 39 | K5 |
| Rempstone Notts | 30 | C7 |
| Renfrew Rens | 45 | H2 |
| Renwick Cumb | 42 | D7 |
| Repton Derbys | 29 | K6 |
| Resolven Neath | 19 | L6 |
| Retford Notts | 30 | D2 |
| Reynoldston Swans | 19 | H7 |
| Rhayader Powys | 20 | D4 |
| Rhiconich Highld | 63 | H3 |
| Rhoose V Glam | 5 | J2 |

| | | | |
|---|---|---|---|
| Rhosllanerchrugog | | |
| Wrexhm | 27 | L5 |
| Rhosneigr IoA | 26 | C3 |
| Rhôs-on-Sea Conwy | 27 | G2 |
| Rhossili Swans | 19 | G7 |
| Rhu Ag & B | 49 | L5 |
| Rhuddlan Denbgs | 27 | J3 |
| Rhyd-Ddu Gwynd | 26 | E4 |
| Rhydowen Cerdgn | 19 | G2 |
| Rhyl Denbgs | 27 | H2 |
| Rhymney Caerph | 12 | C1 |
| Richards Castle | | |
| Herefs | 21 | J4 |
| Richmond Gt Lon | 15 | J6 |
| Richmond N York | 38 | B3 |
| Rickmansworth | | |
| Herts | 15 | H4 |
| Riding Mill Nthumb | 43 | H5 |
| Ridsdale Nthumb | 43 | G4 |
| Rillington N York | 39 | H5 |
| Ringford D & G | 41 | G6 |
| Ringmer E Susx | 10 | C6 |
| Ringwood Hants | 8 | C5 |
| Ripley Derbys | 29 | K5 |
| Ripley N York | 38 | C7 |
| Ripley Surrey | 15 | H7 |
| Ripon N York | 38 | D6 |
| Ripple Worcs | 21 | M6 |
| Ripponden Calder | 33 | J5 |
| Risca Caerph | 12 | D3 |
| Risegate Lincs | 31 | H6 |
| Riseley Bed | 23 | K4 |
| Riseley Wokham | 14 | E7 |
| Risley Derbys | 29 | L6 |
| Risley Warrtn | 32 | F7 |
| Roade Nhants | 23 | H5 |
| Roberton Border | 46 | E7 |
| Roberton S Lans | 45 | M5 |
| Robertsbridge E Susx | 10 | F6 |
| Robeston Wathen | | |
| Pembks | 18 | E5 |
| Robin Hood's Bay | | |
| N York | 39 | J3 |
| Rocester Staffs | 29 | H6 |
| Roch Pembks | 18 | C4 |
| Rochdale Rochdl | 33 | H5 |
| Roche Cnwll | 2 | F4 |
| Rochester Medway | 10 | F2 |
| Rochester Nthumb | 42 | F3 |
| Rochford Essex | 17 | G7 |
| Rock Cnwll | 2 | F3 |
| Rockcliffe Cumb | 42 | B5 |
| Rockcliffe D & G | 41 | J6 |
| Rockingham Nhants | 23 | J2 |
| Rogate W Susx | 9 | H4 |
| Rogerstone Newpt | 12 | D3 |
| Rollesby Norfk | 25 | L4 |
| Rolvenden Kent | 11 | G5 |
| Romaldkirk Dur | 37 | M2 |
| Romanno Bridge | | |
| Border | 46 | C5 |
| Romford Gt Lon | 16 | D7 |
| Romsey Hants | 8 | D4 |
| Rookhope Dur | 43 | G7 |
| Ropley Hants | 9 | G3 |
| Rosedale Abbey | | |
| N York | 39 | G4 |
| Rosehall Highld | 63 | K7 |
| Rosehearty Abers | 61 | G3 |
| Rosemarkie Highld | 58 | F4 |
| Rosewell Mdloth | 46 | D4 |
| Rossett Wrexhm | 28 | B4 |
| Ross-on-Wye Herefs | 21 | K7 |
| Rosyth Fife | 46 | B2 |
| Rothbury Nthumb | 43 | H2 |
| Rotherfield E Susx | 10 | D5 |
| Rotherham Rothm | 34 | B7 |
| Rothes Moray | 59 | L4 |
| Rothesay Ag & B | 49 | J6 |
| Rothwell Leeds | 33 | M4 |
| Rothwell Nhants | 23 | J2 |
| Rottingdean Br & H | 10 | C7 |
| Roughton Norfk | 25 | J3 |
| Rowland's Castle | | |
| Hants | 9 | G5 |
| Rowlands Gill Gatesd | 43 | J6 |
| Rowsley Derbys | 29 | J3 |
| Roxburgh Border | 47 | G6 |
| Roxwell Essex | 16 | E6 |
| Royal Leamington | | |
| Spa Warwks | 22 | D4 |
| Royal Sutton | | |
| Coldfield Birm | 22 | C3 |
| Royal Tunbridge | | |
| Wells Kent | 10 | E4 |
| Royal Wootton | | |
| Bassett Wilts | 13 | L3 |
| Royston Barns | 34 | A5 |
| Royston Herts | 16 | C4 |
| Rozel Jersey | 7 | c1 |
| Ruabon Wrexhm | 27 | L4 |
| Ruddington Notts | 30 | C6 |

| | | | |
|---|---|---|---|
| Rudgwick W Susx | 9 | K3 |
| Rudston E R Yk | 39 | K6 |
| Rufford Lancs | 32 | D5 |
| Rugby Warwks | 22 | F3 |
| Rugeley Staffs | 29 | G7 |
| Rumbling Bridge | | |
| P & K | 50 | F6 |
| Runcorn Halton | 28 | C2 |
| Rushden Nhants | 23 | K4 |
| Rushyford Dur | 38 | C1 |
| Ruskington Lincs | 31 | G5 |
| Rustington W Susx | 9 | K5 |
| Ruswarp N York | 39 | H3 |
| Rutherglen S Lans | 45 | J2 |
| Ruthin Denbgs | 27 | J4 |
| Ruyton-XI-Towns | | |
| Shrops | 28 | B7 |
| Rydal Cumb | 37 | G3 |
| Ryde IoW | 8 | F6 |
| Rye E Susx | 11 | G6 |

| | | | |
|---|---|---|---|
| **S** | | |
| Saddell Ag & B | 44 | B5 |
| Saffron Walden | | |
| Essex | 16 | D4 |
| St Abbs Border | 47 | J3 |
| St Agnes Cnwll | 2 | D5 |
| St Albans Herts | 15 | H3 |
| St Andrew Guern | 6 | a2 |
| St Andrews Fife | 51 | K5 |
| St Arvans Mons | 12 | F2 |
| St Asaph Denbgs | 27 | J3 |
| St Athan V Glam | 5 | J1 |
| St Aubin Jersey | 7 | b2 |
| St Austell Cnwll | 2 | F5 |
| St Bees Cumb | 36 | D3 |
| St Blazey Cnwll | 3 | G5 |
| St Boswells Border | 46 | F6 |
| St Brelade Jersey | 7 | a2 |
| St Brelade's Bay | | |
| Jersey | 7 | a2 |
| St Briavels Gloucs | 12 | F2 |
| St Buryan Cnwll | 2 | A7 |
| St Catherines Ag & B | 49 | J3 |
| St Clears Carmth | 18 | F5 |
| St Cleer Cnwll | 3 | H4 |
| St Clement Jersey | 7 | c2 |
| St Columb Major | | |
| Cnwll | 2 | F4 |
| St Combs Abers | 61 | H3 |
| St Cyrus Abers | 55 | K7 |
| St Davids Pembks | 18 | B4 |
| St Day Cnwll | 2 | D6 |
| St Dogmaels Pembks | 18 | E2 |
| St Fergus Abers | 61 | H4 |
| St Fillans P & K | 50 | C4 |
| St Florence Pembks | 18 | E6 |
| St Helens IoW | 9 | G6 |
| St Helens St Hel | 32 | E7 |
| St Helier Jersey | 7 | b2 |
| St Ives Cambs | 24 | A8 |
| St Ives Cnwll | 2 | B6 |
| St John Jersey | 7 | b1 |
| St John's IoM | 36 | b3 |
| St John's Chapel Dur | 43 | G7 |
| St John's Town of | | |
| Dalry D & G | 41 | G4 |
| St Jude's IoM | 36 | c2 |
| St Just Cnwll | 2 | A7 |
| St Just-in-Roseland | | |
| Cnwll | 2 | E7 |
| St Keverne Cnwll | 2 | E8 |
| St Keyne Cnwll | 3 | H5 |
| St Lawrence IoW | 8 | F7 |
| St Lawrence Jersey | 7 | b1 |
| St Leonards E Susx | 10 | F7 |
| St Margaret's at | | |
| Cliffe Kent | 11 | L4 |
| St Margaret's Hope | | |
| Ork | 65 | c5 |
| St Marks IoM | 36 | b3 |
| St Martin Guern | 6 | b2 |
| St Martin Jersey | 7 | c1 |
| St Mary Jersey | 7 | b1 |
| St Mary's Ork | 65 | c4 |
| St Mary's Bay Kent | 11 | J5 |
| St Mawes Cnwll | 2 | E7 |
| St Mawgan Cnwll | 2 | E4 |
| St Monans Fife | 51 | K6 |
| St Neots Cambs | 23 | M4 |
| St Osyth Essex | 17 | J5 |
| St Ouen Jersey | 7 | a1 |
| St Owens Cross | | |
| Herefs | 21 | J7 |
| St Peter Jersey | 7 | b1 |
| St Peter Port Guern | 6 | b2 |
| St Peter's Guern | 6 | a2 |
| St Sampson Guern | 6 | b1 |
| St Saviour Guern | 6 | a2 |

| Place | County | Page | Grid |
|---|---|---|---|
| St Saviour | Jersey | 7 | b2 |
| St Stephen | Cnwll | 2 | F5 |
| St Tudy | Cnwll | 3 | G3 |
| Salcombe | Devon | 6 | B7 |
| Sale | Traffd | 33 | G7 |
| Salen | Ag & B. | 52 | D6 |
| Salen | Highld | 52 | E4 |
| Salford | Salfd | 33 | G6 |
| Salfords | Surrey | 10 | B4 |
| Saline | Fife | 50 | F7 |
| Salisbury | Wilts | 8 | C3 |
| Saltash | Cnwll | 3 | K5 |
| Saltburn-by-the-Sea | R & Cl | 38 | F2 |
| Saltcoats | N Ayrs | 44 | F4 |
| Saltfleet | Lincs | 35 | K7 |
| Sampford Arundel | Somset | 5 | K5 |
| Sanaigmore | Ag & B. | 48 | B6 |
| Sandbach | Ches E. | 28 | E4 |
| Sandbank | Ag & B | 49 | K5 |
| Sandford-on-Thames | Oxon | 14 | C4 |
| Sandhaven | Abers | 61 | G3 |
| Sandhead | D & G | 40 | C6 |
| Sandhurst | Br For. | 14 | F7 |
| Sandness | Shet | 61 | a5 |
| Sandon | Staffs | 29 | G6 |
| Sandown | IoW | 8 | F7 |
| Sandridge | Herts | 15 | J3 |
| Sandsend | N York | 39 | H3 |
| Sandwich | Kent | 11 | L3 |
| Sandwick | Shet | 61 | c7 |
| Sandy | C Beds | 23 | L5 |
| Sanquhar | D & G | 45 | L6 |
| Sarn | Gwynd | 26 | B6 |
| Sarre | Kent | 11 | K2 |
| Saundby | Notts | 34 | E7 |
| Saundersfoot | Pembks | 18 | E5 |
| Saunton | Devon | 4 | D4 |
| Sawbridgeworth | Herts | 16 | D5 |
| Sawston | Cambs | 16 | D3 |
| Sawtry | Cambs | 23 | L3 |
| Saxby | Leics | 30 | E7 |
| Saxilby | Lincs | 30 | E3 |
| Saxmundham | Suffk | 17 | L2 |
| Saxthorpe | Norfk | 25 | H3 |
| Scalasaig | Ag & B. | 48 | C4 |
| Scalby | N York | 39 | J4 |
| Scalloway | Shet | 61 | c6 |
| Scamblesby | Lincs | 31 | J3 |
| Scarborough | N York | 39 | K4 |
| Scarinish | Ag & B | 48 | b2 |
| Scawby | N Linc | 34 | F6 |
| Scole | Norfk | 25 | H7 |
| Scone | P & K | 51 | G4 |
| Sconser | Highld | 56 | E6 |
| Scotch Corner | N York | 38 | C3 |
| Scotter | Lincs | 34 | F6 |
| Scotton | N York | 38 | B4 |
| Scoulton | Norfk | 25 | G5 |
| Scourie | Highld | 63 | G4 |
| Scrabster | Highld | 65 | G2 |
| Scunthorpe | N Linc | 34 | F5 |
| Seaford | E Susx | 10 | D7 |
| Seahouses | Nthumb | 47 | L6 |
| Seal | Kent | 10 | D3 |
| Seamer | N York | 39 | J5 |
| Sea Palling | Norfk | 25 | L3 |
| Seascale | Cumb | 36 | D3 |
| Seathwaite | Cumb | 36 | F4 |
| Seaton | Cumb | 41 | K8 |
| Seaton | Devon | 6 | F3 |
| Seaton Delaval | Nthumb | 43 | K4 |
| Seave Green | N York | 38 | F4 |
| Seaview | IoW | 9 | G6 |
| Sedbergh | Cumb | 37 | J4 |
| Sedgeberrow | Worcs | 22 | B6 |
| Sedgebrook | Lincs | 30 | E6 |
| Sedgefield | Dur | 38 | D1 |
| Sedlescombe | E Susx | 10 | F6 |
| Seend | Wilts | 13 | K5 |
| Selborne | Hants | 9 | G3 |
| Selby | N York | 34 | D4 |
| Selkirk | Border | 46 | E6 |
| Sellindge | Kent | 11 | J4 |
| Selsey | W Susx | 9 | H6 |
| Selston | Notts | 29 | L4 |
| Send | Surrey | 15 | G7 |
| Sennen | Cnwll | 2 | A7 |
| Sennybridge | Powys | 20 | D7 |
| Setchey | Norfk | 24 | D4 |
| Settle | N York | 37 | L6 |
| Sevenoaks | Kent | 10 | D3 |
| Seven Sisters | Neath | 19 | L5 |
| Shaftesbury | Dorset | 13 | J8 |
| Shalford | Essex | 16 | F4 |
| Shalford | Surrey | 9 | K2 |
| Shandon | Ag & B | 49 | K5 |
| Shanklin | IoW | 8 | F7 |
| Shap | Cumb | 37 | H2 |
| Shardlow | Derbys | 29 | L6 |
| Sharnbrook | Bed | 23 | K4 |
| Sharpness | Gloucs | 13 | G2 |
| Shaugh Prior | Devon | 3 | L4 |
| Shavington | Ches E. | 28 | E5 |
| Shawbury | Shrops | 28 | C7 |
| Shebbear | Devon | 4 | D6 |
| Sheepwash | Devon | 4 | E6 |
| Sheerness | Kent | 11 | G2 |
| Sheffield | Sheff | 29 | K2 |
| Shefford | C Beds | 23 | L6 |
| Shepreth | Cambs | 16 | C3 |
| Shepshed | Leics | 30 | B7 |
| Shepton Mallet | Somset | 13 | G6 |
| Sherborne | Dorset | 7 | J1 |
| Sherburn | N York | 39 | J5 |
| Sherburn in Elmet | N York | 34 | C4 |
| Sherfield on Loddon | Hants | 14 | D7 |
| Sheriff Hutton | N York | 38 | F6 |
| Sheringham | Norfk | 25 | H2 |
| Shiel Bridge | Highld | 57 | J7 |
| Shieldaig | Highld | 57 | H4 |
| Shifnal | Shrops | 28 | E8 |
| Shildon | Dur | 38 | C2 |
| Shillingford | Oxon | 14 | D4 |
| Shillingford | Dorset | 7 | L2 |
| Shinfield | Wokham | 14 | E6 |
| Shinness | Highld | 63 | K6 |
| Shipdham | Norfk | 25 | G5 |
| Shiplake | Oxon | 14 | E6 |
| Shipley | C Brad. | 33 | K3 |
| Shipston-on-Stour | Warwks | 22 | D6 |
| Shipton | N York | 38 | E7 |
| Shiptonthorpe | E R Yk. | 34 | E3 |
| Shirebrook | Derbys | 30 | B3 |
| Shoeburyness | Sthend | 17 | G8 |
| Shoreham-by-Sea | W Susx | 9 | L5 |
| Shorwell | IoW | 8 | E7 |
| Shotley | Suffk | 17 | K4 |
| Shottisham | Suffk | 17 | L3 |
| Shotts | N Lans | 45 | L2 |
| Shrewsbury | Shrops | 28 | C8 |
| Shrewton | Wilts | 13 | L6 |
| Shrivenham | Oxon | 13 | M3 |
| Shurdington | Gloucs | 22 | A7 |
| Shute | Devon | 6 | F3 |
| Sible Hedingham | Essex | 16 | F4 |
| Sibsey | Lincs | 31 | J5 |
| Sibson | Leics | 22 | E1 |
| Sidmouth | Devon | 6 | E3 |
| Silchester | Hants | 14 | D7 |
| Sileby | Leics | 30 | C7 |
| Silk Willoughby | Lincs | 31 | G5 |
| Silloth | Cumb | 41 | L6 |
| Silsoe | C Beds | 23 | L6 |
| Silverdale | Lancs | 37 | H5 |
| Silver End | Essex | 16 | F5 |
| Silverstone | Nhants | 23 | G6 |
| Silverton | Devon | 5 | H6 |
| Simonburn | Nthumb | 42 | F4 |
| Simonsbath | Somset | 5 | G4 |
| Singleton | W Susx | 9 | J4 |
| Sissinghurst | Kent | 10 | F4 |
| Sittingbourne | Kent | 11 | G3 |
| Sixpenny Handley | Dorset | 8 | A4 |
| Skegness | Lincs | 31 | L4 |
| Skellingthorpe | Lincs | 30 | E3 |
| Skelmersdale | Lancs | 32 | D6 |
| Skelmorlie | N Ayrs | 49 | K6 |
| Skelton | Cumb | 42 | C7 |
| Skelton | R & Cl | 38 | F2 |
| Skenfrith | Mons. | 21 | H7 |
| Skerray | Highld | 64 | C2 |
| Skipness | Ag & B. | 44 | C3 |
| Skipsea | E R Yk. | 35 | H2 |
| Skipton | N York | 33 | J2 |
| Skirling | Border | 46 | B6 |
| Skirwith | Cumb | 42 | D8 |
| Slaidburn | Lancs | 32 | F2 |
| Slaley | Nthumb | 43 | G6 |
| Slamannan | Falk | 45 | L1 |
| Slapton | Devon | 6 | B7 |
| Sleaford | Lincs | 31 | G5 |
| Sledmere | E R Yk | 39 | J6 |
| Sleights | N York | 39 | H3 |
| Slingsby | N York | 39 | G5 |
| Slough | Slough | 15 | G5 |
| Smailholm | Border | 47 | G6 |
| Smarden | Kent | 11 | G4 |
| Smithfield | Cumb | 42 | C5 |
| Snainton | N York | 39 | J5 |
| Snape | Suffk | 17 | L2 |
| Snettisham | Norfk | 24 | E3 |
| Snodland | Kent | 10 | E3 |
| Soham | Cambs | 24 | D7 |
| Solihull | Solhll | 22 | C3 |
| Solva | Pembks | 18 | B4 |
| Somersham | Cambs | 24 | B7 |
| Somerton | Somset | 12 | F7 |
| Sompting | W Susx | 9 | L5 |
| Sonning | Wokham | 14 | E6 |
| Sonning Common | Oxon | 14 | E5 |
| Sorbie | D & G | 40 | E6 |
| Soulby | Cumb | 37 | K3 |
| Souldern | Oxon | 22 | F6 |
| Souldrop | Bed | 23 | K4 |
| Sourton | Devon | 3 | J1 |
| Southam | Warwks | 22 | E4 |
| Southampton | C Sotn | 8 | E5 |
| South Benfleet | Essex | 16 | F8 |
| Southborough | Kent | 10 | D4 |
| South Brent | Devon | 6 | A5 |
| South Cave | E R Yk | 34 | F4 |
| South Elmsall | Wakefd | 34 | B5 |
| Southend | Ag & B. | 44 | B6 |
| Southend-on-Sea | Sthend | 17 | G8 |
| Southery | Norfk | 24 | D6 |
| South Harting | W Susx | 9 | H4 |
| South Hayling | Hants | 9 | G5 |
| South Holmwood | Surrey | 9 | L2 |
| South Kyme | Lincs | 31 | H5 |
| South Mimms | Herts | 15 | J4 |
| Southminster | Essex | 17 | H7 |
| South Molton | Devon | 4 | F5 |
| Southmoor | Oxon | 14 | B4 |
| South Normanton | Derbys | 29 | L4 |
| South Ockendon | Thurr | 16 | E8 |
| South Petherton | Somset | 7 | G1 |
| Southport | Sefton | 32 | C5 |
| South Queensferry | C Edin | 46 | B3 |
| South Raynham | Norfk | 24 | F4 |
| Southrepps | Norfk | 25 | J3 |
| Southsea | C Port | 9 | G6 |
| South Shields | S Tyne | 43 | L5 |
| South Stainley | N York | 38 | C6 |
| South Walsham | Norfk | 25 | K4 |
| Southwell | Notts | 30 | D4 |
| Southwick | Hants | 9 | G5 |
| Southwick | W Susx | 10 | B7 |
| South Witham | Lincs | 30 | F7 |
| Southwold | Suffk | 25 | L7 |
| South Woodham Ferrers | Essex | 16 | F7 |
| South Zeal | Devon | 3 | M2 |
| Sowerby | N York | 38 | D5 |
| Sowerby Bridge | Calder | 33 | J4 |
| Spalding | Lincs | 31 | H7 |
| Sparkford | Somset | 13 | G8 |
| Sparsholt | Hants | 8 | E3 |
| Spean Bridge | Highld | 53 | J3 |
| Spennymoor | Dur | 43 | K7 |
| Spetisbury | Dorset | 7 | L2 |
| Spey Bay | Moray | 60 | B3 |
| Spilsby | Lincs | 31 | K3 |
| Spinningdale | Highld | 58 | F1 |
| Spittal | Highld | 65 | H3 |
| Spittal of Glenshee | P & K | 54 | E7 |
| Spixworth | Norfk | 25 | J4 |
| Spofforth | N York | 34 | A2 |
| Springholm | D & G | 41 | H5 |
| Sproatley | E R Yk | 35 | H4 |
| Stadhampton | Oxon | 14 | D4 |
| Stadhlaigearraidh | W Isls | 62 | c11 |
| Staffin | Highld | 56 | E3 |
| Stafford | Staffs | 28 | F7 |
| Staindrop | Dur | 38 | B2 |
| Staines-upon-Thames | Surrey | 15 | G6 |
| Stainforth | N York | 37 | L1 |
| Staithes | N York | 39 | G2 |
| Stalham | Norfk | 25 | K4 |
| Stalybridge | Tamesd | 33 | J6 |
| Stamford | Lincs | 31 | G8 |
| Stamford Bridge | E R Yk | 39 | G7 |
| Stamfordham | Nthumb | 43 | H5 |
| Standish | Wigan | 32 | E5 |
| Standon | Herts | 16 | C5 |
| Stanford in the Vale | Oxon | 14 | B4 |
| Stanford le Hope | Thurr | 10 | E1 |
| Stanhope | Dur | 43 | G7 |
| Stanley | Dur | 43 | J6 |
| Stanley | P & K | 50 | F4 |
| Stannington | Nthumb | 43 | J4 |
| Stansted Mountfitchet | Essex | 16 | D5 |
| Stanton | Suffk | 25 | G7 |
| Stanton St Quintin | Wilts | 13 | J4 |
| Stanway | Gloucs | 22 | B6 |
| Staple Fitzpaine | Somset | 6 | F1 |
| Stapleford | Notts | 30 | B6 |
| Staplehurst | Kent | 10 | F4 |
| Starbotton | N York | 37 | M5 |
| Staveley | Cumb | 37 | H4 |
| Staveley | Derbys | 29 | L3 |
| Staverton | Nhants | 22 | F4 |
| Staxton | N York | 39 | J5 |
| Steeple | Essex | 17 | G6 |
| Steeple Aston | Oxon | 22 | F7 |
| Steeple Bumpstead | Essex | 16 | E3 |
| Stenhousemuir | Falk | 50 | B8 |
| Steornabhagh | W Isls | 62 | h3 |
| Stevenage | Herts | 16 | B5 |
| Stevenston | N Ayrs | 44 | F4 |
| Steventon | Oxon | 14 | C5 |
| Stewarton | E Ayrs | 45 | H3 |
| Stewkley | Bucks | 23 | J7 |
| Steyning | W Susx | 9 | L5 |
| Stibb Cross | Devon | 4 | D5 |
| Stickford | Lincs | 31 | J4 |
| Stickney | Lincs | 31 | J4 |
| Stiffkey | Norfk | 25 | G2 |
| Stilligarry | W Isls | 62 | c11 |
| Stillington | N York | 38 | F6 |
| Stilton | Cambs | 23 | L2 |
| Stirling | Stirlg | 50 | D7 |
| Stock | Essex | 16 | E7 |
| Stockbridge | Hants | 8 | D3 |
| Stockport | Stockp | 33 | H7 |
| Stocksbridge | Sheff | 33 | L6 |
| Stockton-on-Tees | S on T | 38 | E2 |
| Stogursey | Somset | 12 | C6 |
| Stoke-by-Clare | Suffk | 16 | F3 |
| Stoke-by-Nayland | Suffk | 17 | H4 |
| Stoke Canon | Devon | 6 | C3 |
| Stoke Ferry | Norfk | 24 | E5 |
| Stoke Fleming | Devon | 6 | C6 |
| Stoke Gabriel | Devon | 6 | C6 |
| Stoke Goldington | M Keyn | 23 | J5 |
| Stoke Lacy | Herefs | 21 | K5 |
| Stoke Mandeville | Bucks | 14 | F3 |
| Stokenchurch | Bucks | 14 | E4 |
| Stoke-on-Trent | C Stke | 28 | F5 |
| Stoke Poges | Bucks | 15 | G5 |
| Stokesley | N York | 38 | E3 |
| Stone | Staffs | 28 | F6 |
| Stonehaven | Abers | 55 | L5 |
| Stonehouse | Gloucs | 13 | H2 |
| Stonehouse | S Lans | 45 | K3 |
| Stoneykirk | D & G | 40 | B6 |
| Stonor | Oxon | 14 | E5 |
| Stony Stratford | M Keyn | 23 | H6 |
| Stornoway | W Isls | 62 | h3 |
| Storrington | W Susx | 9 | K4 |
| Stotfold | C Beds | 16 | A4 |
| Stoulton | Worcs | 22 | A5 |
| Stourbridge | Dudley | 21 | M3 |
| Stourpaine | Dorset | 7 | L2 |
| Stourport-on-Severn | Worcs | 21 | L3 |
| Stourton | Staffs | 21 | M2 |
| Stow | Border | 46 | E5 |
| Stow-cum-Quy | Cambs | 16 | D2 |
| Stowmarket | Suffk | 17 | H2 |
| Stow-on-the-Wold | Gloucs | 22 | C7 |
| Strachan | Abers | 55 | K5 |
| Strachur | Ag & B. | 49 | J3 |
| Stradbroke | Suffk | 25 | J7 |
| Stradishall | Suffk | 16 | F3 |
| Stradsett | Norfk | 24 | D5 |
| Straiton | S Ayrs | 45 | G7 |
| Stranraer | D & G | 40 | B5 |
| Stratfield Turgis | Hants | 14 | E7 |

| Place | County | Page | Grid |
|---|---|---|---|
| Stratford | Gt Lon | 16 | C8 |
| Stratford St Andrew | Suffk | 17 | L2 |
| Stratford-upon-Avon | Warwks | 22 | C5 |
| Strathaven | S Lans | 45 | K4 |
| Strathblane | Stirlg | 50 | B8 |
| Strathcanaird | Highld | 63 | G7 |
| Strathdon | Abers | 55 | G3 |
| Strathpeffer | Highld | 58 | D4 |
| Strathy | Highld | 64 | E2 |
| Strathyre | Stirlg | 50 | B5 |
| Stratton | Cnwll | 4 | B6 |
| Stratton-on-the-Fosse | Somset | 13 | G6 |
| Streatley | W Berk | 14 | D5 |
| Street | Somset | 12 | F7 |
| Strensall | C York | 38 | F7 |
| Strete | Devon | 6 | C6 |
| Stretford | Traffd | 33 | G7 |
| Stretham | Cambs | 24 | C7 |
| Stretton | Rutlnd | 30 | F7 |
| Strichen | Abers | 61 | G4 |
| Stromeferry | Highld | 57 | H5 |
| Stromness | Ork | 65 | b4 |
| Stronachlachar | Stirlg | 49 | M3 |
| Strone | Ag & B | 49 | K5 |
| Strontian | Highld | 52 | F5 |
| Strood | Medway | 10 | F2 |
| Stroud | Gloucs | 13 | J2 |
| Struy | Highld | 58 | C5 |
| Stuartfield | Abers | 61 | G5 |
| Studland | Dorset | 8 | B7 |
| Studley | Warwks | 22 | B4 |
| Sturminster Newton | Dorset | 7 | K1 |
| Sturry | Kent | 11 | J3 |
| Sturton by Stow | Lincs | 30 | E2 |
| Sudbury | Derbys | 29 | H6 |
| Sudbury | Suffk | 17 | G3 |
| Sulby | IoM | 36 | c2 |
| Summercourt | Cnwll | 2 | E5 |
| Sunbury-on-Thames | Surrey | 15 | H6 |
| Sunderland | Sundld | 43 | L6 |
| Surfleet | Lincs | 31 | H6 |
| Sutterton | Lincs | 31 | J6 |
| Sutton | Cambs | 24 | C7 |
| Sutton | Gt Lon | 10 | B2 |
| Sutton Benger | Wilts | 13 | K4 |
| Sutton Bridge | Lincs | 24 | C4 |
| Sutton Coldfield | Birm | 22 | C2 |
| Sutton Courtenay | Oxon | 14 | C4 |
| Sutton-in-Ashfield | Notts | 30 | B4 |
| Sutton on Sea | Lincs | 31 | L2 |
| Sutton-on-the-Forest | N York | 38 | F6 |
| Sutton on Trent | Notts | 30 | E3 |
| Sutton Scotney | Hants | 8 | E2 |
| Sutton Valence | Kent | 10 | F4 |
| Swadlincote | Derbys | 29 | K7 |
| Swaffham | Norfk | 24 | F5 |
| Swainswick | BaNES | 13 | H4 |
| Swalcliffe | Oxon | 22 | E6 |
| Swallow | Lincs | 35 | H6 |
| Swallowfield | Wokham | 14 | E7 |
| Swanage | Dorset | 8 | B7 |
| Swanley | Kent | 10 | D2 |
| Swansea | Swans | 19 | J6 |
| Swanwick | Derbys | 29 | K4 |
| Swanwick | Hants | 8 | F5 |
| Swaton | Lincs | 31 | G6 |
| Swavesey | Cambs | 16 | C1 |
| Sway | Hants | 8 | D6 |
| Swindon | Wilts | 13 | L3 |
| Swineshead | Bed | 23 | K4 |
| Swineshead | Lincs | 31 | H5 |
| Swinford | Leics | 22 | F3 |
| Swinton | Border | 47 | H5 |
| Swinton | Rothm | 34 | B6 |
| Syderstone | Norfk | 24 | F3 |
| Symbister | Shet | 61 | d4 |
| Symington | S Ayrs | 45 | G5 |
| Symington | S Lans | 46 | A6 |
| Symonds Yat (West) | Herefs | 21 | J8 |
| Syresham | Nhants | 23 | G6 |
| Syston | Leics | 30 | C8 |

## T

| Place | County | Page | Grid |
|---|---|---|---|
| Tadcaster | N York | 34 | B3 |
| Tadley | Hants | 14 | D7 |
| Tain | Highld | 59 | G2 |
| Tairbeart | W Isls | 62 | f6 |
| Talgarreg | Cerdgn | 19 | G2 |
| Talgarth | Powys | 20 | F6 |
| Talladale | Highld | 57 | J3 |
| Talley | Carmth | 19 | J3 |
| Talmine | Highld | 64 | C2 |
| Talsarnau | Gwynd | 26 | E6 |
| Tal-y-Bont | Cerdgn | 20 | B2 |
| Tal-y-Bont | Conwy | 26 | F3 |
| Tal-y-bont | Gwynd | 26 | E7 |
| Tal-y-Cafn | Conwy | 27 | G3 |
| Tamworth | Staffs | 22 | C1 |
| Tannadice | Angus | 51 | J2 |
| Tan-y-groes | Cerdgn | 18 | F2 |
| Taplow | Bucks | 14 | F5 |
| Tarbert | Ag & B | 49 | G6 |
| Tarbert | W Isls | 62 | f6 |
| Tarbet | Ag & B | 49 | L3 |
| Tarbolton | S Ayrs | 45 | H5 |
| Tarland | Abers | 55 | H4 |
| Tarleton | Lancs | 32 | D5 |
| Tarporley | Ches W | 28 | C4 |
| Tarrant Hinton | Dorset | 7 | M2 |
| Tarskavaig | Highld | 56 | F7 |
| Tarves | Abers | 60 | F6 |
| Tarvin | Ches W | 28 | C3 |
| Tattershall | Lincs | 31 | H4 |
| Taunton | Somset | 12 | D8 |
| Taverham | Norfk | 25 | H4 |
| Tavistock | Devon | 3 | K4 |
| Tayinloan | Ag & B | 44 | B3 |
| Taynton | Oxon | 22 | D8 |
| Taynuilt | Ag & B | 53 | G7 |
| Tayport | Fife | 51 | J4 |
| Tayvallich | Ag & B | 48 | F5 |
| Tebay | Cumb | 37 | J3 |
| Tedburn St Mary | Devon | 6 | B3 |
| Teddington | Gloucs | 22 | A6 |
| Teignmouth | Devon | 6 | C4 |
| Telford | Wrekin | 28 | E8 |
| Temple | Mdloth | 46 | D4 |
| Temple Bar | Cerdgn | 19 | H2 |
| Templecombe | Somset | 13 | H8 |
| Temple Sowerby | Cumb | 37 | J1 |
| Tempsford | C Beds | 23 | L5 |
| Tenbury Wells | Worcs | 21 | K4 |
| Tenby | Pembks | 18 | E6 |
| Tenterden | Kent | 11 | G5 |
| Ternhill | Shrops | 28 | D6 |
| Terrington St Clement | Norfk | 24 | C4 |
| Tetbury | Gloucs | 13 | J3 |
| Tetford | Lincs | 31 | J3 |
| Tetney | Lincs | 35 | J6 |
| Tetsworth | Oxon | 14 | E4 |
| Teviothead | Border | 42 | C2 |
| Tewkesbury | Gloucs | 21 | M6 |
| Teynham | Kent | 11 | H3 |
| Thame | Oxon | 14 | E3 |
| Thatcham | W Berk | 14 | C6 |
| Thaxted | Essex | 16 | E4 |
| Theale | W Berk | 14 | D6 |
| Theberton | Suffk | 17 | M2 |
| The Bungalow | IoM | 36 | c2 |
| Thetford | Norfk | 24 | F7 |
| Theydon Bois | Essex | 16 | C7 |
| Thirsk | N York | 38 | D5 |
| Thornbury | S Glos | 13 | G3 |
| Thorne | Donc | 34 | D5 |
| Thorney | C Pete | 24 | A5 |
| Thornham | Norfk | 24 | E2 |
| Thornhill | D & G | 41 | J3 |
| Thornhill | Stirlg | 50 | C6 |
| Thornley | Dur | 43 | L7 |
| Thornton | Fife | 51 | H6 |
| Thornton-le-Dale | N York | 39 | H5 |
| Thornton-le-Street | N York | 38 | D7 |
| Thornton Watlass | N York | 38 | C5 |
| Thorpe End | Norfk | 25 | J5 |
| Thorpe-le-Soken | Essex | 17 | J5 |
| Thorpeness | Suffk | 17 | M2 |
| Thorrington | Essex | 17 | J5 |
| Thrapston | Nhants | 23 | K3 |
| Three Cocks | Powys | 20 | F6 |
| Threekingham | Lincs | 31 | G6 |
| Threlkeld | Cumb | 36 | F2 |
| Threshfield | N York | 37 | M6 |
| Thropton | Nthumb | 43 | H2 |
| Thrumster | Highld | 65 | J4 |
| Thurcroft | Rothm | 34 | C7 |
| Thurlestone | Devon | 6 | A7 |
| Thurnscoe | Barns | 34 | B6 |
| Thursby | Cumb | 42 | B6 |
| Thurso | Highld | 65 | G2 |
| Thurstaston | Wirral | 27 | K2 |
| Thurston | Suffk | 17 | G2 |
| Thwaite | N York | 37 | L4 |
| Tibshelf | Derbys | 29 | L4 |
| Ticehurst | E Susx | 10 | E5 |
| Tickhill | Donc | 34 | C7 |
| Ticknall | Derbys | 29 | K7 |
| Tideswell | Derbys | 29 | H3 |
| Tidworth | Wilts | 8 | C2 |
| Tigh a Ghearraidh | W Isls | 62 | c8 |
| Tigharry | W Isls | 62 | c8 |
| Tilbury | Thurr | 10 | E2 |
| Tilford | Surrey | 9 | J2 |
| Tillicoultry | Clacks | 50 | E6 |
| Tilshead | Wilts | 13 | K6 |
| Tilstock | Shrops | 28 | C6 |
| Tilton on the Hill | Leics | 30 | D8 |
| Tintagel | Cnwll | 3 | G3 |
| Tintern Parva | Mons | 12 | F2 |
| Tiptree | Essex | 17 | G5 |
| Tisbury | Wilts | 13 | K7 |
| Tissington | Derbys | 29 | J5 |
| Tittensor | Staffs | 28 | F6 |
| Tiverton | Devon | 5 | H6 |
| Tobermory | Ag & B | 52 | C5 |
| Toddington | C Beds | 23 | K7 |
| Todmorden | Calder | 33 | H4 |
| Toft | Shet | 61 | c3 |
| Toft Hill | Dur | 38 | B1 |
| Tolastadh | W Isls | 62 | i2 |
| Tollard Royal | Wilts | 7 | M1 |
| Tollesbury | Essex | 17 | H6 |
| Tolleshunt D'Arcy | Essex | 17 | G6 |
| Tolpuddle | Dorset | 7 | K3 |
| Tolsta | W Isls | 62 | i2 |
| Tomatin | Highld | 59 | G6 |
| Tomintoul | Moray | 54 | F3 |
| Tomnavoulin | Moray | 59 | K6 |
| Tonbridge | Kent | 10 | E4 |
| Tongue | Highld | 64 | C3 |
| Tonypandy | Rhondd | 12 | B3 |
| Tonyrefail | Rhondd | 12 | B3 |
| Topcliffe | N York | 38 | D5 |
| Topsham | Devon | 6 | D3 |
| Torbeg | N Ayrs | 44 | C5 |
| Torcross | Devon | 6 | B7 |
| Tore | Highld | 58 | E4 |
| Torksey | Lincs | 30 | E3 |
| Torphichen | W Loth | 46 | A3 |
| Torphins | Abers | 55 | J4 |
| Torpoint | Cnwll | 3 | K5 |
| Torquay | Torbay | 6 | C5 |
| Torrance | E Duns | 45 | J1 |
| Torridon | Highld | 57 | H4 |
| Torrin | Highld | 56 | F7 |
| Torryburn | Fife | 46 | B2 |
| Torthorwald | D & G | 41 | K4 |
| Torver | Cumb | 36 | F4 |
| Totland | IoW | 8 | D6 |
| Totnes | Devon | 6 | B5 |
| Totton | Hants | 8 | D4 |
| Towcester | Nhants | 23 | G5 |
| Tow Law | Dur | 43 | J7 |
| Town Yetholm | Border | 47 | H6 |
| Traquair | Border | 46 | D6 |
| Trawden | Lancs | 33 | H3 |
| Trawsfynydd | Gwynd | 26 | F6 |
| Trearddur Bay | IoA | 26 | B2 |
| Trecastle | Powys | 20 | D7 |
| Tredegar | Blae G | 12 | C1 |
| Treen | Cnwll | 2 | A8 |
| Trefriw | Conwy | 27 | G4 |
| Tregaron | Cerdgn | 19 | J1 |
| Tregony | Cnwll | 2 | F6 |
| Treherbert | Rhondd | 19 | M6 |
| Trellech | Mons | 12 | F2 |
| Tremadog | Gwynd | 26 | E5 |
| Trimdon | Dur | 43 | L7 |
| Trimingham | Norfk | 25 | J3 |
| Tring | Herts | 14 | F3 |
| Trinity | Jersey | 7 | b1 |
| Troon | S Ayrs | 45 | G5 |
| Trotton | W Susx | 9 | H4 |
| Troutbeck | Cumb | 37 | G3 |
| Trowbridge | Wilts | 13 | J5 |
| Truro | Cnwll | 2 | E6 |
| Tugby | Leics | 23 | H1 |
| Tullibody | Clacks | 50 | D7 |
| Tummel Bridge | P & K | 50 | D2 |
| Tunbridge Wells | Kent | 10 | E4 |
| Tunstall | Suffk | 17 | L2 |
| Turnberry | S Ayrs | 44 | F7 |
| Turnditch | Derbys | 29 | K5 |
| Turner's Hill | W Susx | 10 | B5 |
| Turriff | Abers | 60 | E4 |
| Turvey | Bed | 23 | K5 |
| Tutbury | Staffs | 29 | J6 |
| Tuxford | Notts | 30 | D3 |
| Twycross | Leics | 22 | E1 |
| Twyford | Hants | 8 | E4 |
| Twyford | Wokham | 14 | E6 |
| Twynholm | D & G | 41 | G6 |
| Tyndrum | Stirlg | 53 | K7 |
| Tynemouth | N Tyne | 43 | L5 |
| Tytherleigh | Devon | 6 | F2 |
| Tywyn | Gwynd | 20 | A1 |

## U

| Place | County | Page | Grid |
|---|---|---|---|
| Uckfield | E Susx | 10 | D6 |
| Uffculme | Devon | 5 | J6 |
| Uffington | Oxon | 14 | A5 |
| Ugborough | Devon | 6 | A6 |
| Uig | Highld | 56 | D3 |
| Ulceby | N Linc | 35 | H5 |
| Uldale | Cumb | 42 | A7 |
| Ullapool | Highld | 63 | G7 |
| Ullenhall | Warwks | 22 | C4 |
| Ulpha | Cumb | 36 | E4 |
| Ulsta | Shet | 61 | c3 |
| Ulverston | Cumb | 36 | F5 |
| Umberleigh | Devon | 4 | F5 |
| Unapool | Highld | 63 | H4 |
| Upavon | Wilts | 13 | L5 |
| Uplyme | Devon | 6 | F3 |
| Upminster | Gt Lon | 16 | D8 |
| Upottery | Devon | 6 | E2 |
| Upper Beeding | W Susx | 9 | L5 |
| Upper Benefield | Nhants | 23 | K2 |
| Upper Broughton | Notts | 30 | D7 |
| Upper Largo | Fife | 51 | J6 |
| Upper Lydbrook | Gloucs | 21 | K8 |
| Upper Tean | Staffs | 29 | G5 |
| Uppingham | Rutlnd | 23 | J1 |
| Upstreet | Kent | 11 | K3 |
| Upton Snodsbury | Worcs | 22 | A5 |
| Upton-upon-Severn | Worcs | 21 | M6 |
| Urchfont | Wilts | 13 | K5 |
| Usk | Mons | 12 | E2 |
| Uttoxeter | Staffs | 29 | H6 |
| Uxbridge | Gt Lon | 15 | H5 |
| Uyeasound | Shet | 61 | d2 |

## V

| Place | County | Page | Grid |
|---|---|---|---|
| Vale | Guern | 6 | b1 |
| Ventnor | IoW | 8 | F7 |
| Verwood | Dorset | 8 | B5 |
| Vidlin | Shet | 61 | c4 |
| Virginia Water | Surrey | 15 | G6 |
| Voe | Shet | 61 | c4 |

## W

| Place | County | Page | Grid |
|---|---|---|---|
| Waddesdon | Bucks | 14 | E3 |
| Waddington | Lancs | 33 | G3 |
| Waddington | Lincs | 30 | F4 |
| Wadebridge | Cnwll | 2 | F4 |
| Wadesmill | Herts | 15 | K3 |
| Wadhurst | E Susx | 10 | E5 |
| Wainfleet All Saints | Lincs | 31 | K4 |
| Wakefield | Wakefd | 33 | M5 |
| Walberswick | Suffk | 25 | L7 |
| Walgherton | Ches E | 28 | E5 |
| Walkerburn | Border | 46 | D6 |
| Walkern | Herts | 16 | B5 |
| Walkington | E R Yk | 35 | G3 |
| Wallasey | Wirral | 32 | C7 |
| Wallingford | Oxon | 14 | D5 |
| Walls | Shet | 61 | b5 |
| Walsall | Wsall | 22 | B1 |
| Waltham | NE Lin | 35 | J6 |
| Waltham Abbey | Essex | 16 | C7 |
| Waltham on the Wolds | Leics | 30 | D7 |
| Walton | Powys | 21 | G4 |
| Walton | Somset | 12 | F7 |
| Walton-on-Thames | Surrey | 15 | H6 |
| Walton-on-the-Naze | Essex | 17 | K5 |
| Wanlockhead | D & G | 45 | L6 |
| Wansford | C Pete | 23 | L1 |
| Wanstrow | Somset | 13 | H6 |
| Wantage | Oxon | 14 | B5 |
| Warboys | Cambs | 24 | A7 |

Warcop Cumb.............37 K2
Wardlow Derbys.........29 J3
Ware Herts.................15 K3
Wareham Dorset..........7 L3
Warenford Nthumb.....47 L6
Wargrave Wokham .....14 E6
Wark Nthumb.............42 H4
Wark Nthumb.............47 H6
Warkworth Nthumb....43 K2
Warlingham Surrey.....10 C3
Warmington Warwks...22 E5
Warminster Wilts.......13 J6
Warninglid W Susx....10 B5
Warrington Warrtn.....32 F7
Warsash Hants..............8 E5
Warslow Staffs...........29 H4
Warton Lancs.............32 D4
Warwick Warwks........22 D4
Wasbister Ork.............65 b2
Wasdale Head Cumb...36 E3
Washingborough
  Lincs........................30 F3
Washington Sundld....43 K6
Watchet Somset...........5 J3
Watchgate Cumb........37 H4
Waterbeach Cambs.....16 D2
Waterbeck D & G........42 A4
Waterhouses Staffs....29 H5
Waterlooville Hants.....9 G5
Watermillock Cumb....37 G2
Watford Herts.............15 H4
Watford Nhants..........23 G4
Wath upon Dearne
  Rothm......................34 B6
Watlington Oxon.........14 E4
Watten Highld............65 H3
Watton Norfk.............24 F5
Watton-at-Stone
  Herts........................15 K2
Wearhead Dur............42 F7
Weasenham All
  Saints Norfk.............24 F4
Weaverham Ches W....28 D3
Wedmore Somset........12 E6
Weedon Bec Nhants....23 G4
Week St Mary Cnwll.....4 B7
Weem P & K...............50 D2
Welbourn Lincs..........30 F4
Wellesbourne
  Warwks....................22 D5
Wellingborough
  Nhants......................23 J4
Wellington Somset.......5 K5
Wellington Wrekin.....28 D8
Wells Somset..............12 F6
Wells-next-the-Sea
  Norfk........................24 F2
Welney Norfk.............24 C6
Welshampton Shrops..28 B6
Welshpool Powys........27 K8
Welton Nhants............23 G4
Welwyn Herts.............15 J3
Welwyn Garden City
  Herts........................15 J3
Wem Shrops...............28 C6
Wembley Gt Lon.........15 J5
Wembury Devon...........3 L6
Wendover Bucks.........14 F3
Wensley N York.........38 B4
Wentbridge Wakefd....34 B5
Weobley Herefs..........21 H5
Wereham Norfk..........24 D5
West Auckland Dur....38 B2
West Bay Dorset..........7 H3
West Bexington
  Dorset.......................7 H3
West Bilney Norfk......24 E4
West Bridgford
  Notts........................30 C6
West Bromwich
  Sandw......................22 B2
Westbury Shrops........28 B8
Westbury Wilts...........13 J6
West Calder W Loth....46 A4
West Chiltington
  W Susx.......................9 K4
Westcott Surrey...........9 L2
Westerham Kent.........10 C3
West Felton Shrops.....27 L7
Westfield E Susx.........10 F6
Westgate-on-Sea
  Kent.........................11 L2
West Haddon Nhants..23 G3
Westhill Abers...........55 L4
West Hoathly W Susx..10 C5
West Horsley Surrey...15 H8
West Huntspill
  Somset......................12 D6
West Kilbride N Ayrs..44 F3
West Kirby Wirral.......27 K2
West Lavington Wilts..13 K6
West Linton Border.....46 C5

West Lulworth
  Dorset........................7 L4
West Lynn Norfk........24 D4
West Malling Kent......10 E3
West Malvern Worcs...21 L5
West Meon Hants.........9 G4
West Mersea Essex.....17 H6
West Moors Dorset.......8 B5
Westnewton Cumb......41 L7
West Newton Norfk....24 E3
Weston Herts.............16 B4
Weston Staffs.............29 G6
Westonbirt Gloucs......13 J3
Weston Heath
  Shrops......................28 E7
Weston-on-the-
  Green Oxon..............14 C3
Weston-sub-Edge
  Gloucs......................22 C6
Weston-super-Mare
  N Som.......................12 D5
Weston-under-
  Redcastle Shrops......28 D6
West Pennard
  Somset......................12 F7
West Pentire Cnwll.......2 D5
West Rounton N York..38 D3
West Runton Norfk.....25 J2
Westruther Border......47 G5
West Sandwick Shet....61 c3
Westward Ho!
  Devon.........................4 D4
West Wittering
  W Susx.......................9 H6
West Witton N York....38 A4
West Woodburn
  Nthumb....................43 G3
Wetheral Cumb..........42 C6
Wetherby Leeds.........34 B3
Wetwang E R Yk.........39 J7
Weybourne Norfk.......25 H2
Weybridge Surrey.......15 H7
Weyhill Hants..............8 D2
Weymouth Dorset........7 J4
Whaley Bridge
  Derbys......................29 G2
Whalley Lancs............33 G3
Whaplode Lincs..........31 J7
Whaplode Drove
  Lincs........................31 J7
Whauphill D & G........40 E6
Wheathampstead
  Herts........................15 J3
Wheatley Oxon...........14 D3
Wheddon Cross
  Somset........................5 H4
Whepstead Suffk........17 G2
Wherwell Hants...........8 E2
Whickham Gatesd......43 J5
Whiddon Down
  Devon.........................6 A3
Whimple Devon............6 D3
Whipsnade C Beds......15 G3
Whitburn W Loth......46 A4
Whitby N York............39 H3
Whitchurch Bucks......14 E2
Whitchurch Hants........8 E2
Whitchurch Herefs.....21 J8
Whitchurch Shrops.....28 C5
Whitebridge Highld....58 D7
Whitehaven Cumb......36 D2
Whitehill and
  Bordon Hants.............9 H3
Whitehills Abers.........60 D3
Whitehouse Ag & B....49 G6
Whitekirk E Loth........46 F2
Whitewell Lancs.........32 F3
Whithorn D & G.........40 E7
Whiting Bay N Ayrs....44 E5
Whitland Carmth........18 E5
Whitley Bay N Tyne....43 K5
Whitley Chapel
  Nthumb....................43 G6
Whitminster Gloucs....13 H1
Whitstable Kent.........11 J2
Whittington Shrops....27 L6
Whittlebury Nhants....23 G6
Whittlesey Cambs......24 A6
Whitton Powys...........21 G4
Whitwell Derbys.........30 B3
Whitwell Herts...........15 J2
Wick Highld...............65 J3
Wickford Essex...........16 F7
Wickham Hants...........8 F5
Wickham Market
  Suffk........................17 K2
Wickwar S Glos..........13 H3
Widdrington
  Nthumb....................43 K3
Widecombe in the
  Moor Devon................6 A4
Widegates Cnwll..........3 J5

Widemouth Bay
  Cnwll.........................4 B6
Widford Herts............16 C5
Widmerpool Notts......30 C6
Widnes Halton...........28 C2
Wigan Wigan.............32 E6
Wiggenhall St
  Germans Norfk.........24 D4
Wigston Leics............23 G1
Wigton Cumb............42 A6
Wigtown D & G..........40 E6
Wilberfoss E R Yk......34 D2
Wilby Nhants.............23 J4
Willand Devon.............5 J6
Willingham Cambs.....24 B8
Williton Somset...........5 J3
Wilmcote Warwks......22 C4
Wilmington Devon.......6 F2
Wilmslow Ches E.......28 F2
Wilsontown S Lans.....46 A4
Wilstead Bed.............23 L6
Wilton Wilts..............13 L7
Wimbledon Gt Lon....15 J6
Wimblington Cambs...24 B6
Wimborne Minster
  Dorset........................8 A5
Wincanton Somset.....13 H7
Winchcombe Gloucs...22 B7
Winchelsea E Susx.....11 G6
Winchester Hants.........8 E3
Windermere Cumb......37 G4
Windsor W & M..........15 G6
Wing Bucks...............14 F2
Wingate Dur..............43 L7
Wingham Kent...........11 K3
Winkfield Br For........14 F6
Winkleigh Devon..........4 F6
Winscombe N Som.....12 E5
Winsford Ches W........28 D3
Winsford Somset..........5 H4
Winsham Somset.........7 G2
Winslow Bucks...........23 H7
Winster Derbys...........29 J4
Winterborne
  Monkton Dorset.........7 J3
Winterborne
  Stickland Dorset........7 L2
Winterborne
  Whitechurch
  Dorset........................7 L2
Winterbourne
  Abbas Dorset..............7 J3
Winterbourne Stoke
  Wilts........................13 L7
Winteringham N Linc..34 F5
Winterslow Wilts.........8 C3
Winterton N Linc.......34 F5
Winwick Cambs.........23 L3
Wirksworth Derbys....29 J4
Wisbech Cambs..........31 K8
Wisborough Green
  W Susx.......................9 K3
Wishaw N Lans..........45 L3
Witham Essex............16 F3
Witheridge Devon........5 G6
Withern Lincs.............31 K2
Withernsea E R Yk.....35 K4
Withington Gloucs.....22 B8
Withington Herefs.....21 J6
Withyham E Susx.......10 D5
Withypool Somset........5 H4
Witnesham Suffk........17 J3
Witney Oxon..............14 B3
Wittersham Kent........11 G5
Witton le Wear Dur....43 J8
Wiveliscombe
  Somset........................5 J4
Wivelsfield E Susx.....10 C6
Wivenhoe Essex.........17 H5
Wix Essex...................17 J4
Woburn C Beds..........23 K6
Woburn Sands
  M Keyn.....................23 J6
Woking Surrey...........15 G7
Wokingham Wokham..14 F6
Wolf's Castle Pembks..18 C4
Wollaston Nhants.......23 J4
Wollaston Shrops.......27 L8
Wolsingham Dur........43 H7
Wolverhampton
  Wolves......................21 M1
Wolvey Warwks.........22 E2
Wolviston S on T.......38 E2
Wombourne Staffs.....21 M2
Wombwell Barns........34 B6
Wooburn Bucks..........14 F5
Woodborough Suffk...17 K3
Woodchurch Kent......11 G5
Woodford Gloucs.......13 G2
Woodhall Spa Lincs....31 H4
Woodland Dur............38 B2
Woodstock Oxon.........14 C3

Woofferton Shrops.....21 J4
Wookey Hole Somset..12 F6
Wool Dorset................7 L3
Woolacombe Devon.....4 D3
Wooler Nthumb.........47 K6
Woolhampton
  W Berk......................14 D6
Woolpit Suffk.............17 H2
Woolwich Gt Lon.......10 C1
Woore Shrops............28 E5
Wootton N Linc.........35 G5
Wootton Oxon............14 B2
Wootton Bassett
  Wilts........................13 L3
Wootton Courtenay
  Somset........................5 H3
Wootton Wawen
  Warwks....................22 C4
Worcester Worcs........21 M5
Workington Cumb......36 D1
Worksop Notts...........30 C2
Worlingworth Suffk....17 K1
Wormit Fife...............51 J4
Worplesdon Surrey.....15 G7
Worthen Shrops..........21 G1
Worthing W Susx.........9 L5
Worth Matravers
  Dorset........................7 M4
Wotton-under-Edge
  Gloucs......................13 H3
Wragby Lincs.............31 G3
Wrangaton Devon........6 A6
Wrangle Lincs............31 K5
Wrawby N Linc..........35 G6
Wrelton N York..........39 G5
Wrentham Suffk.........25 L7
Wrestlingworth
  C Beds......................16 B3
Wrexham Wrexhm.....27 L5
Wrexham Industrial
  Estate Wrexhm.........28 B5
Writtle Essex.............16 E6
Wroughton Swindn....13 L4
Wroxall IoW................8 F7
Wroxeter Shrops........28 D8
Wroxham Norfk.........25 K4
Wroxton Oxon...........22 E6
Wyboston Bed...........23 L5
Wye Kent...................11 H4
Wylye Wilts...............13 K7
Wymeswold Leics......30 E7
Wymondham Norfk....25 H5

**Y**

Yarcombe Devon..........6 F2
Yardley Gobion
  Nhants......................23 H5
Yardley Hastings
  Nhants......................23 J5
Yarm S on T..............38 D3
Yarmouth IoW.............8 D6
Yarrowford Border......46 E6
Yate S Glos................13 H3
Yateley Hants............14 F7
Yatton N Som............12 E5
Yatton Keynell Wilts..13 J4
Yaxley Cambs............23 M2
Yeadon Leeds............33 K3
Yealmpton Devon........3 L5
Yelverton Devon..........3 L4
Yelverton Norfk.........25 K5
Yeovil Somset.............7 H1
Yeovilton Somset.......12 F8
Yetts o'Muckhart
  Clacks......................50 E6
Y Felinheli Gwynd.....26 D3
Y Maerdy Conwy.......27 J5
York C York...............34 C2
Youlgreave Derbys....29 J4
Yoxall Staffs..............29 H7
Yoxford Suffk.............17 L1
Y Rhiw Gwynd...........26 B6
Ysbyty Ystwyth
  Cerdgn......................20 B3
Ystalyfera Neath........19 K5
Ystradgynlais Powys..19 K5
Ystrad Mynach
  Caerph......................12 C2

**Z**

Zeals Wilts................13 H7
Zennor Cnwll...............2 B6

This chart shows distances in miles
between two towns along AA-recommended
routes. Using motorways and other main roads this
is normally the fastest route, though not necessarily
the shortest.

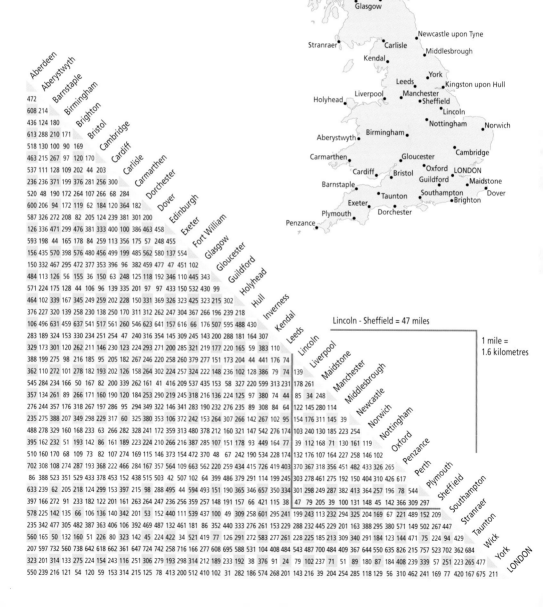

Lincoln - Sheffield = 47 miles

1 mile =
1.6 kilometres

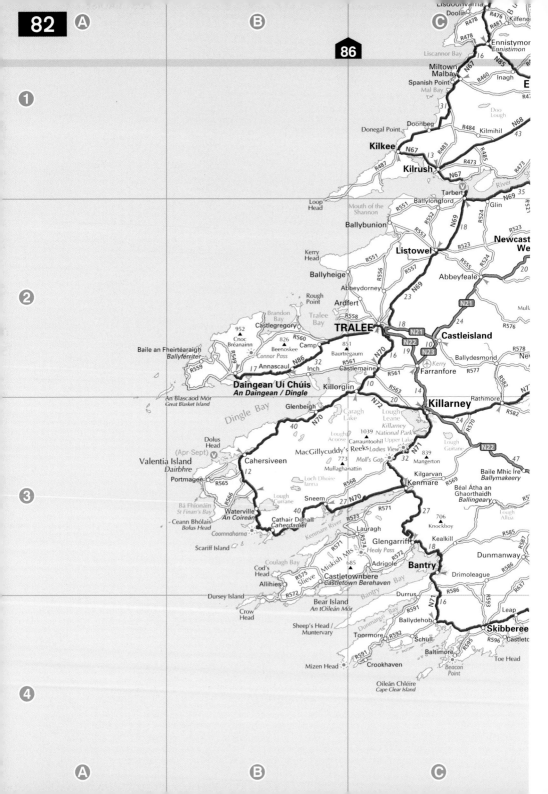

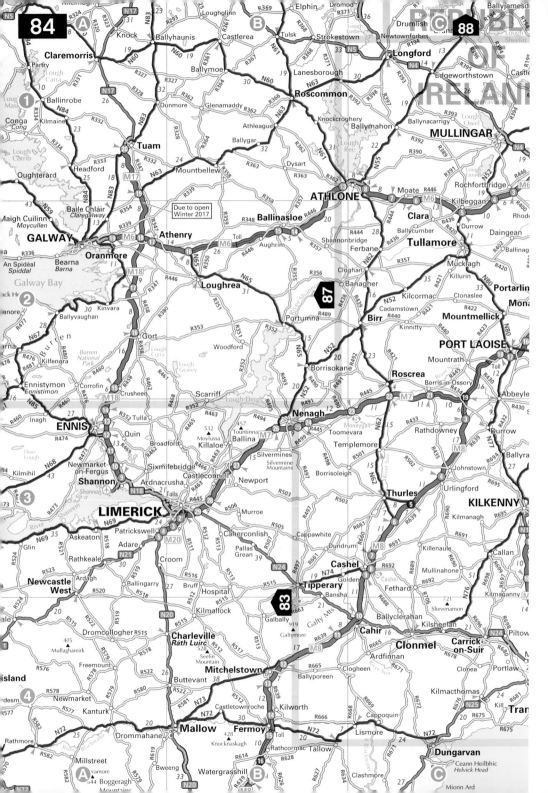

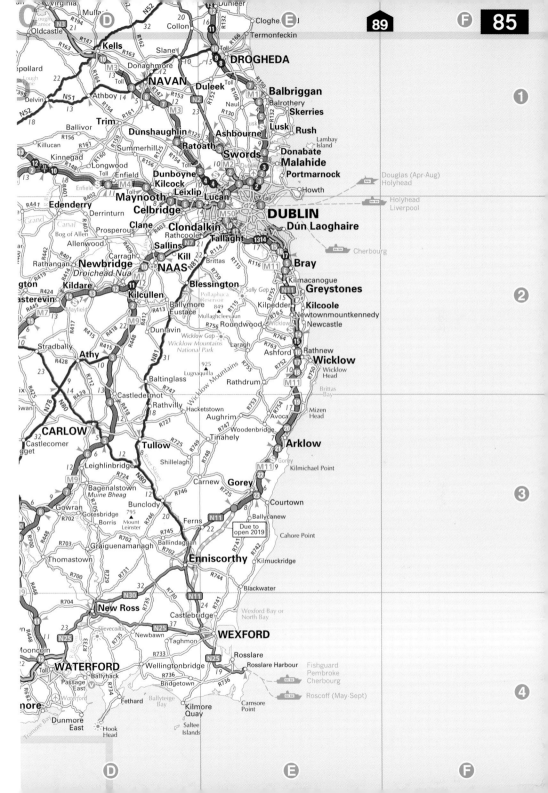

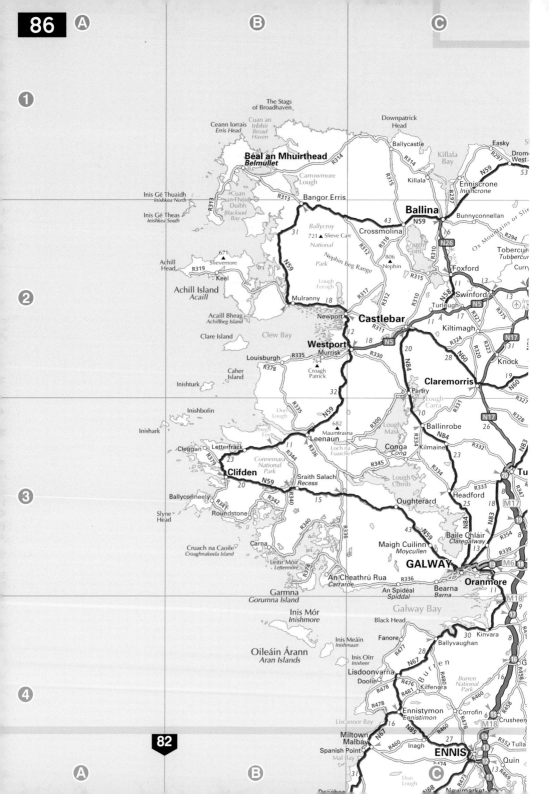

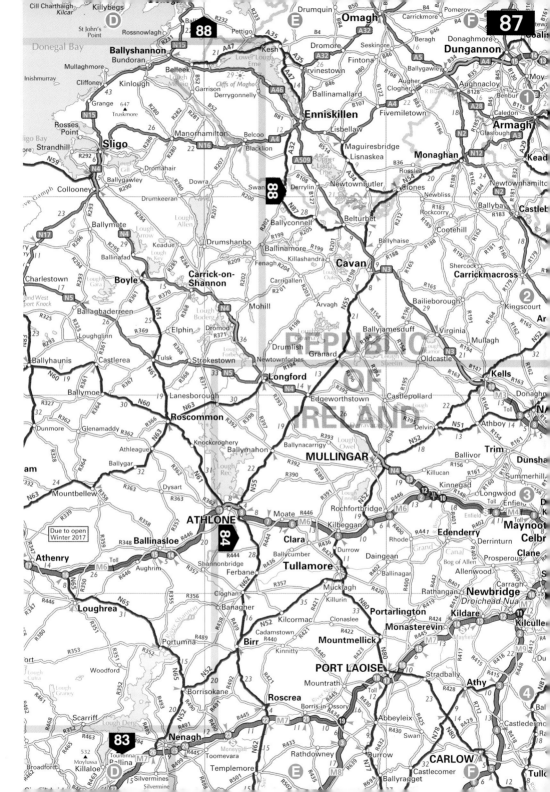

This chart shows distances, in both miles and kilometres, between two towns along AA-recommended routes. Using motorways and other main roads this is normally the fastest route, though not always the shortest.

For example, the distance between Clifden and Mullingar is 206 kilometres or 128 miles (8 kilometres is approximately 5 miles).

To reflect the distances shown on road signs, distances shown on the road maps in this atlas are in miles in Northern Ireland and kilometres in the Republic of Ireland.

## Distances in miles

The chart is a triangular distance matrix between Irish towns, listed diagonally: Antrim, Armagh, Athlone, Ballina, Bantry, Belfast, Carlow, Castlebar, Cavan, Clifden, Coleraine, Cork, Daingean Uí Chúis / An Daingean / Dingle, Donegal, Downpatrick, Dublin, Dundalk, An Clochán Liath / Dunglow / Dungloe, Ennis, Enniskillen, Galway, Ireland West Airport Knock, Kilkee, Kilkenny, Killarney, Larne, Limerick, Londonderry / Derry, Mullingar, Omagh, Port Laoise, Roscommon, Rosslare, Sligo, Tipperary, Tralee, Tullamore, Waterford, Wexford, Wicklow.

Distances in miles (upper right of diagonal):

```
42 150 153 322 18 165 169 99 221 38 332 105 93 38 114 60 106 221 75 203 150 255 190 301 22 235 54 119 53 166 143 208 116 227 296 153 215 193 143
99 127 290 40 134 143 48 194 60 239 294 74 52 81 29 94 170 47 150 124 204 158 269 63 203 70 91 36 134 101 176 90 195 263 121 183 162 111
83 181 149 72 81 51 101 157 130 64 114 150 76 106 148 71 81 53 62 105 78 139 171 73 133 29 101 48 20 126 74 86 134 24 110 117 106
231 160 153 24 101 75 150 184 216 76 171 147 140 112 104 79 70 30 138 160 191 183 124 121 100 103 130 63 208 37 149 186 106 192 199 177
313 163 217 244 218 353 52 84 286 305 209 262 319 132 275 170 216 107 140 43 335 110 326 201 293 157 202 170 246 116 64 176 126 162 205
156 176 97 228 87 262 317 106 22 104 52 201 125 250 190 157 281 181 292 23 226 71 110 164 157 142 199 124 217 286 144 206 162 134
152 117 171 196 111 185 184 148 52 104 219 118 147 124 134 150 24 160 178 94 196 75 68 24 91 55 145 71 155 44 49 46 56
104 52 167 168 200 93 188 146 157 128 88 95 47 29 122 159 51 199 107 137 99 119 107 139 61 206 51 206 51 132 170 104 191 198 175
151 106 192 213 68 108 71 51 103 122 30 103 85 156 142 188 119 122 82 44 49 88 53 168 62 149 82 168 67 153 103
218 168 201 144 239 176 206 179 89 146 48 80 122 158 176 250 108 188 128 170 147 96 225 104 134 170 124 188 216 206
308 359 76 75 152 98 84 229 85 198 149 263 228 339 47 273 32 152 64 204 149 246 115 265 334 175 253 231 181
95 238 253 157 209 273 85 222 122 168 116 89 55 283 62 274 149 241 104 171 118 198 63 75 124 75 110 153
269 309 213 265 304 116 243 153 199 76 173 41 339 93 294 192 273 161 188 207 232 116 31 162 165 200 241
127 147 111 35 158 37 126 73 194 190 246 115 177 46 121 41 159 91 238 40 202 242 139 222 229 180
107 54 137 222 92 202 168 273 173 284 44 218 92 102 80 149 153 191 135 210 278 136 198 176 126
52 169 147 100 128 127 178 78 188 126 122 144 50 111 53 96 97 129 114 183 63 103 82 31
121 198 63 158 137 229 129 240 74 174 94 58 62 105 99 148 104 166 235 93 155 133 82
192 77 158 109 226 244 279 126 211 52 147 58 191 129 270 75 237 274 171 269 255 205
154 42 88 32 105 91 272 24 206 101 173 93 77 144 118 48 86 96 103 136 173
134 75 186 171 217 103 152 52 75 25 118 65 198 213 179 213 98 196 183 132
53 75 111 129 232 61 167 80 152 100 48 178 83 86 123 76 140 169 158
121 140 174 180 106 117 80 99 109 42 188 34 132 168 86 172 179 157
137 64 303 55 239 134 206 125 110 175 151 80 45 130 134 167 204
127 203 81 221 76 188 98 98 62 152 53 142 51 31 54 87
314 68 270 167 237 135 164 160 204 91 21 141 119 152 216
248 75 132 74 179 163 221 146 240 309 166 228 206 156
205 103 172 71 99 120 137 25 63 76 79 112 151
126 33 170 117 240 84 231 264 150 247 226 175
93 45 45 128 81 106 162 25 107 119 79
137 89 208 66 198 232 117 214 193 142
68 78 122 62 130 21 63 70 80
145 55 107 158 43 130 137 126
199 96 176 98 44 9 68
162 199 98 184 191 158
85 81 54 88 141
135 134 168 210
83 89 93
37 80
53
```

## Distances in kilometres

Distances in kilometres (lower left of diagonal):

```
68
242 159
246 204 133
518 467 292 374
29 65 239 258 504
266 215 116 241 262 251
272 230 130 39 349 284 245
159 78 82 159 392 156 188 167
355 313 162 121 351 367 276 83 243
61 97 253 242 568 87 316 268 170 351
435 59 209 296 84 421 179 270 309 271 496
169 473 264 348 135 510 298 322 342 323 575 153
150 119 183 180 460 171 296 149 109 231 123 383 433
61 83 241 276 491 35 287 320 192 402 76 456 385 121 407 497 204
183 131 123 237 337 168 84 235 114 283 244 253 343 237 173
97 46 171 225 421 83 168 252 82 331 158 337 427 178 87 83
170 151 239 180 513 201 353 206 165 288 135 439 490 56 222 272 194
356 274 115 168 213 402 190 142 197 143 369 136 186 254 357 236 319 309
120 76 131 127 442 130 236 153 49 235 136 358 391 54 188 161 101 124 248
326 243 85 113 274 306 199 76 166 78 319 196 247 202 325 207 255 254 67 214
241 199 100 48 348 253 215 46 137 128 239 270 321 118 271 205 220 175 141 121 85
410 328 169 222 172 452 241 196 251 197 423 186 122 313 439 286 369 363 52 299 121 195
306 255 126 258 226 292 39 256 229 255 367 143 278 306 279 125 208 393 169 276 178 226 220
484 433 224 308 70 470 257 282 302 283 545 88 66 396 457 303 387 449 147 350 207 280 103 204
35 101 275 294 539 37 287 320 192 402 76 456 546 176 374 289 488 327 505 374 206 359 488 547
378 327 118 199 177 364 152 173 196 174 439 99 120 502 285 351 197 281 340 38 245 98 171 88 131 110 399
87 113 214 194 525 114 316 220 132 302 51 441 474 74 148 231 152 83 331 83 269 189 384 356 434 120 330
191 147 46 161 323 177 121 159 71 206 244 240 309 195 164 80 93 237 162 120 129 129 216 122 269 212 165 203
86 58 162 165 472 110 264 191 79 274 103 389 440 66 128 179 100 94 278 40 245 160 332 303 381 119 277 53 150
267 215 77 209 252 252 39 207 142 237 328 168 259 256 239 86 157 350 161 50 218 288 114 274 72 221
230 162 32 101 325 228 147 98 85 154 239 276 303 147 246 155 159 208 124 104 77 68 177 158 264 263 159 188 72 143 109
335 284 202 334 273 321 88 332 271 362 396 190 333 383 308 156 238 435 232 318 286 302 282 100 258 356 193 387 206 334 126 234
187 145 119 59 396 199 234 85 100 168 185 319 373 65 217 207 167 121 190 67 134 54 243 245 329 235 221 135 130 107 196 88 321
365 314 139 240 186 350 114 213 239 215 426 102 187 325 338 184 267 381 78 42 138 212 129 85 146 386 40 371 170 319 99 172 154 261
476 424 215 299 103 461 273 273 293 274 537 121 50 389 448 295 378 441 138 342 198 271 73 228 34 497 102 425 260 373 210 255 283 321 137
246 195 39 172 298 267 79 221 168 109 199 281 200 251 149 275 155 158 122 138 308 130 218
346 295 177 309 203 332 79 307 269 302 407 120 266 357 319 165 249 433 165 342 225 277 216 50 192 367 127 398 173 345 101 209 71 296 87 216 133
311 260 188 320 260 260 74 318 245 348 372 177 322 369 284 132 214 411 219 294 272 288 269 87 245 332 181 363 192 310 112 220 15 308 141 270 144 59
230 178 171 285 330 215 90 282 166 331 291 246 388 289 202 50 132 330 279 213 255 329 140 347 251 243 281 127 229 129 202 110 255 227 338 149 128 86
```

This index lists places appearing in the main-map section of the atlas in alphabetical order. The reference following each name gives the atlas page number and grid reference of the square in which the place appears. The map shows government districts (Northern Ireland), counties and administrative districts, together with a list of the abbreviated name forms used in the index.

## Northern Ireland Districts

| | |
|---|---|
| A & ND | **Ards and North Down** |
| A & N | **Antrim & Newtownabbey** |
| AB & C | **Armagh City, Banbridge & Craigavon** |
| Belfst | **Belfast (1)** |
| CC & G | **Causeway Coast & Glens** |
| D & S | **Derry City & Strabane** |
| E Antr | **Mid & East Antrim** |
| F & O | **Fermanagh & Omagh** |
| L & C | **Lisburn & Castlereagh City** |
| M Ulst | **Mid Ulster** |
| NM & D | **Newry, Mourne and Down** |

## Republic of Ireland

| | | | |
|---|---|---|---|
| C Cork | **Cork City (2)** | Limrck | **Limerick (City &** |
| C Dubl | **Dublin City (3)** | | **County)** |
| C Gal | **Galway City (4)** | Longfd | **Longford** |
| Carlow | **Carlow** | Louth | **Louth** |
| Cavan | **Cavan** | Mayo | **Mayo** |
| Clare | **Clare** | Meath | **Meath** |
| Cork | **Cork** | Monhan | **Monaghan** |
| Donegl | **Donegal** | Offaly | **Offaly** |
| Dublin | **Dublin (Dún** | Roscom | **Roscommon** |
| | **Laoghaire-Rathdown/** | Sligo | **Sligo** |
| | **Fingal/South Dublin)** | Tippry | **Tipperary** |
| Galway | **Galway** | Watfd | **Waterford (City &** |
| Kerry | **Kerry** | | **County)** |
| Kildre | **Kildare** | Wmeath | **Westmeath** |
| Kilken | **Kilkenny** | Wexfd | **Wexford** |
| Laois | **Laois** | Wicklw | **Wicklow** |
| Leitrm | **Leitrim** | | |

## A

Abbeydorney Kerry .... 82 C2
Abbeyfeale Limrck ..... 82 C2
Adare Limrck .............. 83 D2
Adrigole Cork.............. 82 C3
Aghalee L & C............. 89 D3
Ahoghill E Antr .......... 89 D2
Allenwood Kildre......... 85 D2
Allihies Cork ............... 82 B3
An Bun Beag
  Donegl.................... 88 B2
An Charraig Donegl .... 88 A2
An Cheathrú Rua
  Galway................... 86 B3
An Clochán Liath
  Donegl.................... 88 A2
An Coireán Kerry ........ 82 B3
An Daingean Kerry...... 82 B2
Annahilt L & C............ 89 E3
Annalong NM & D........ 89 E4
Annascaul Kerry .......... 82 B2
An Spidéal Galway ...... 86 C3
Antrim A & N............... 89 D2
Ardagh Limrck ............ 83 D2
Ardara Donegl ............ 88 A2
Ardee Louth ............... 89 D4
Ardfert Kerry............... 82 C2
Ardfinnan Tippry......... 84 C4
Ardglass NM & D......... 89 E3
Ardmore Watfd ........... 83 E3
Ardnacrusha Clare...... 83 D1
Arklow Wicklw ............ 85 E3
Armagh AB & C........... 89 D3
Armoy CC & G............. 89 D1
Arvagh Cavan.............. 88 B4
Ashbourne Meath ....... 85 E1
Ashford Wicklw........... 85 E2
Askeaton Limrck.......... 83 D1
Athboy Meath.............. 85 D1
Athenry Galway........... 87 D3
Athleague Roscom ...... 87 D3
Athlone Wmeath ......... 84 C1
Athy Kildre ................. 85 D2
Augher M Ulst............. 88 C3
Aughnacloy M Ulst...... 88 C3
Aughrim Galway.......... 87 D3
Aughrim Wicklw.......... 85 E3
Avoca Wicklw ............. 85 E3

## B

Bagenalstown
  Carlow..................... 85 D3
Baile an
  Fheirtéaraigh
  Kerry...................... 82 B2
Baile Chláir Galway ..... 86 C3
Baile Mhic Íre Cork..... 82 C3
Bailieborough
  Cavan.................... 88 C4
Balbriggan Dublin ...... 85 E1
Ballaghaderreen
  Roscom.................. 87 D2
Ballina Mayo.............. 86 C2
Ballina Tippry ............ 83 D1
Ballinafad Sligo ......... 87 D2
Ballinagar Offaly........ 84 C2
Ballinamallard F & O... 88 B3
Ballinamore Leitrm...... 87 E2
Ballinasloe Galway...... 87 D3
Ballincollig Cork......... 83 D3
Ballindaggan Wexfd.... 85 D3

Ballingarry Limrck........ 83 D2
Ballingeary Cork ......... 82 C3
Ballinrobe Mayo.......... 86 C3
Ballinspittle Cork ........ 83 D3
Ballintra Donegl .......... 88 B3
Ballivor Meath ............ 85 D1
Ballybay Monhan ........ 88 C4
Ballybofey Donegl........ 88 B2
Ballybunion Kerry ....... 82 C2
Ballycanew Wexfd ....... 85 E3
Ballycarry E Antr ......... 89 E2
Ballycastle CC & G....... 89 D1
Ballycastle Mayo.......... 86 C1
Ballyclare A & N........... 89 E2
Ballyclerahan Tippry.... 84 C4
Ballyconneely
  Galway................... 86 B3
Ballyconnell Cavan...... 88 B4
Ballycotton Cork.......... 83 E3
Ballycumber Offaly...... 84 C2
Ballydehob Cork ......... 82 C4
Ballydesmond Cork..... 82 C2
Ballyferriter Kerry........ 82 B2
Ballygally E Antr.......... 89 E2
Ballygar Galway .......... 87 D3
Ballygawley M Ulst...... 88 C3
Ballygawley Sligo........ 87 D1
Ballygowan A & ND ..... 89 E3
Ballyhack Wexfd ......... 85 D4
Ballyhaise Cavan......... 88 C4
Ballyhalbert A & ND.... 89 E3
Ballyhaunis Mayo........ 87 D2
Ballyheige Kerry.......... 82 B2
Ballyjamesduff
  Cavan.................... 88 C4
Ballylongford Kerry .... 82 C2
Ballymahon Longfd..... 84 C1
Ballymakeery Cork ...... 82 C3
Ballymena E Antr ....... 89 D2
Ballymoe Galway......... 87 D2
Ballymoney CC & G..... 89 D2
Ballymore Eustace
  Kildre..................... 85 D2
Ballymote Sligo .......... 87 D2
Ballynacarrigy
  Wmeath.................. 84 C1
Ballynahinch
  NM & D................... 89 E3
Ballynure A & N........... 89 E2
Ballyporeen Tippry...... 84 B4
Ballyragget Kilken....... 84 C3
Ballyshannon
  Donegl.................... 87 D1
Ballyvaughan Clare .... 86 C4
Ballywalter A & ND..... 89 E3
Balrothery Dublin ....... 85 E1
Baltimore Cork............ 82 C4
Baltinglass Wicklw...... 85 D2
Banagher Offaly.......... 84 B2
Banbridge AB & C....... 89 D3
Bandon Cork............... 83 D3
Bangor A & ND............ 89 E2
Bangor Erris Mayo....... 86 B2
Bansha Tippry ............ 84 B3
Bantry Cork................. 82 C3
Barna Galway.............. 86 C3
Béal an Mhuirthead
  Mayo...................... 86 B1
Béal Átha an
  Ghaorthaidh
  Cork ....................... 82 C3
Bearna Galway............ 86 C3
Belcoo F & O .............. 87 E1
Belfast Belfst .............. 89 E3
Belgooly Cork.............. 83 D3
Bellaghy M Ulst........... 89 D2

Belleek F & O.............. 87 D1
Belmullet Mayo .......... 86 B1
Belturbet Cavan .......... 88 C4
Benburb M Ulst........... 89 D3
Beragh F & O............... 88 C3
Bessbrook NM & D...... 89 D3
Birr Offaly................... 84 C2
Blacklion Cavan .......... 87 E1
Blackwater Wexfd ....... 85 E3
Blarney Cork............... 83 D3
Blessington Wicklw..... 85 D2
Borris Carlow.............. 85 D3
Borris-in-Ossory
  Laois..................... 84 C2
Borrisokane Tippry ..... 87 D4
Borrisoleigh Tippry ..... 84 C3
Boyle Roscom ............. 87 D2
Bray Wicklw................ 85 E2
Bridgetown Wexfd....... 85 D4
Brittas Dublin ............. 85 E2
Broadford Clare .......... 83 D1
Broughshane E Antr.... 89 D2
Bruff Limrck ............... 83 D2
Bunbeg Donegl........... 88 B2
Bunclody Wexfd.......... 85 D3
Buncrana Donegl........ 88 C1
Bundoran Donegl........ 87 D1
Bunnyconnellan
  Mayo...................... 86 C2
Bushmills CC & G........ 89 D1
Buttevant Cork ........... 83 D2
Bweeng Cork .............. 83 D3

## C

Cadamstown Offaly..... 84 C2
Caherconlish Limrck.... 83 D1
Caherdaniel Kerry....... 82 B3
Cahersiveen Kerry....... 82 B3
Cahir Tippry ............... 84 C4
Caledon M Ulst............ 88 C3
Callan Kilken .............. 84 C3
Camp Kerry................. 82 B2
Carndonagh Donegl.... 88 C1
Cappawhite Tippry...... 83 E1
Cappoquin Watfd........ 84 C4
Carlingford Louth ....... 89 D4
Carlow Carlow............. 85 D3
Carna Galway.............. 86 B3
Carnew Wicklw............ 85 E3
Carnlough E Antr ........ 89 E2
Carragh Kildre............ 85 D2
Carraig Airt Donegl..... 88 B1
Carraroe Galway......... 86 B3
Carrick Donegl............ 88 A2
Carrickart Donegl........ 88 B1
Carrickfergus E Antr.... 89 E2
Carrickmacross
  Monhan.................. 89 D4
Carrickmore F & O ...... 88 C3
Carrick-on-
  Shannon Leitrm ...... 87 D2
Carrick-on-Suir
  Tippry..................... 84 C4
Carrigaline Cork ......... 83 D3
Carrigallen Leitrm....... 88 B4
Carrigtwohill Cork ...... 83 E3
Carryduff L & C........... 89 E3
Cashel Tippry.............. 84 C3
Castlebar Mayo........... 86 C2
Castlebellingham
  Louth ..................... 89 D4
Castleblayney
  Monhan.................. 89 D4
Castlebridge Wexfd .... 85 E4

Castlecomer Kilken ..... 85 D3
Castleconnell Limrck .. 83 D1
Castlederg D & S ........ 88 B2
Castledermot Kildre.... 85 D2
Castlegregory Kerry .... 82 B2
Castleisland Kerry ...... 82 C2
Castlemaine Kerry....... 82 C2
Castlemartyr Cork ...... 83 E3
Castlepollard
  Wmeath.................. 84 C1
Castlerea Roscom ....... 87 D2
Castlerock CC & G ...... 88 C1
Castletownbere
  Cork ....................... 82 B3
Castletownroche
  Cork ....................... 83 D2
Castletownshend
  Cork ....................... 82 C4
Castlewellan
  NM & D................... 89 E3
Cathair Dónall
  Kerry...................... 82 B3
Cavan Cavan............... 88 C4
Celbridge Kildre ......... 85 D2
Charlestown Mayo....... 86 C2
Charleville Cork........... 83 D2
Cill Charthaigh
  Donegl.................... 88 A2
Clady D & S................. 88 C2
Clane Kildre ............... 85 D2
Clara Offaly................ 84 C2
Claregalway
  Galway................... 86 C3
Claremorris Mayo........ 86 C2
Clashmore Watfd ........ 83 E3
Claudy D & S............... 88 C2
Cleggan Galway.......... 86 B3
Clifden Galway............ 86 B3
Cliffoney Sligo............ 87 D1
Cloghan Offaly............ 84 C2
Clogheen Tippry.......... 84 B4
Clogher M Ulst............ 88 C3
Clogherhead Louth...... 89 D4
Clogh Mills CC & G...... 89 D2
Clonakilty Cork........... 83 D4
Clonaslee Laois .......... 84 C2
Clondalkin Dublin........ 85 E2
Clonea Watfd .............. 84 C4
Clones Monhan ........... 88 C3
Clonmany Donegl........ 88 C1
Clonmel Tippry............ 84 C4
Cloyne Cork................ 83 E3
Coachford Cork........... 83 D3
Coagh M Ulst.............. 89 D2
Coalisland M Ulst........ 89 D3
Cobh Cork................... 83 E3
Coleraine CC & G ....... 89 D1
Collon Louth............... 89 D4
Collooney Sligo........... 87 D1
Comber A & ND........... 89 E3
Cong Mayo.................. 86 C3
Conga Mayo................ 86 C3
Convoy Donegl............ 88 B2
Cookstown M Ulst........ 89 D2
Cootehill Cavan........... 88 C4
Cork C Cork ................ 83 D3
Corrofin Clare ............ 86 C4
Courtown Wexfd.......... 85 E3
Craigavon AB & C....... 89 D3
Creeslough Donegl...... 88 B1
Crookhaven Cork......... 82 C4
Crookstown Cork......... 83 D3
Croom Limrck.............. 83 D2
Crosshaven Cork......... 83 E3
Crossmaglen
  NM & D................... 89 D4

Crossmolina Mayo ..... 86  C2
Crumlin A & N ............. 89  D2
Crusheen Clare ........... 86  C4
Culdaff Donegl........... 88  C1
Cullybackey E Antr ..... 89  D2
Culmore D & S............ 88  C2
Curry Sligo.................. 87  D2
Cushendall CC & G...... 89  D1
Cushendun CC & G...... 89  D1

## D

Daingean Offaly........... 84  C2
Daingean Uí Chúis
    Kerry ..................... 82  B2
Delvin Wmeath .......... 85  D1
Derrinturn Kildre ........ 85  D2
Derry D & S................. 88  C2
Derrygonnelly
    F & O ..................... 87  E1
Derrylin F & O ............ 88  B3
Dingle Kerry ............... 82  B2
Doagh A & N .............. 89  D2
Donabate Dublin ........ 85  E1
Donaghadee
    A & ND .................. 89  E2
Donaghmore
    M Ulst.................... 88  C3
Donaghmore
    Meath.................... 85  D1
Donegal Donegl........ 88  B2
Doolin Clare................ 86  C4
Doonbeg Clare............ 82  C1
Downpatrick
    NM & D.................. 89  E3
Dowra Leitrm.............. 87  E1
Draperstown
    M Ulst.................... 89  D2
Drimoleague Cork ...... 82  C3
Drogheda Louth......... 85  E1
Droichead Nua
    Kildre .................... 85  D2
Dromahair Leitrm ...... 87  D1
Dromara L & C ........... 89  E3
Dromcollogher
    Limrck.................... 83  D2
Dromiskin Louth ........ 89  D4
Drommahane Cork ..... 83  D3
Dromod Leitrm........... 87  E2
Dromore AB & C ........ 89  D3
Dromore F & O ........... 88  C3
Dromore West
    Sligo ..................... 86  C1
Drumaness NM & D.... 89  E3
Drumfries Donegl ...... 88  C1
Drumkeeran Leitrm.... 87  D1
Drumlish Longfd ........ 88  B4
Drumquin F & O ......... 88  C3
Drumshanbo
    Leitrm.................... 87  E2
Dublin C Dubl ............ 85  E2
Duleek Meath............. 85  E1
Dunboyne Meath ....... 85  D1
Dundalk Louth............ 89  D4
Dundonald L & C ........ 89  E3
Dundrum Tippry ......... 84  B3
Dunfanaghy Donegl.... 88  B1
Dungannon M Ulst..... 89  D3
Dungarvan Watfd ....... 83  F3
Dungiven CC & G........ 88  C2
Dunglow Donegl ........ 88  A2
Dún Laoghaire
    Dublin ................... 85  E2
Dunlavin Wicklw ........ 85  D2
Dunleer Louth............ 89  D4

Dunloy CC & G............ 89  D2
Dunmanway Cork....... 82  C3
Dunmore Galway ........ 87  D3
Dunmore East
    Watfd .................... 85  D4
Dunshaughlin
    Meath.................... 85  D1
Durrow Laois.............. 84  C3
Durrow Offaly ............ 84  C2
Durrus Cork................ 82  C4
Dysart Roscom .......... 87  D3

## E

Easky Sligo ................ 86  C1
Edenderry Offaly........ 85  D2
Edgeworthstown
    Longfd ................... 84  C1
Eglinton D & S............ 88  C2
Elphin Roscom........... 87  D2
Enfield Meath ............ 85  D1
Ennis Clare................. 83  D1
Enniscorthy
    Wexfd .................... 85  D3
Enniscrone Sligo ........ 86  C1
Enniskean Cork .......... 83  D3
Enniskillen F & O........ 88  B3
Ennistymon Clare ...... 86  C4

## F

Fanore Clare .............. 86  C4
Farranfore Kerry ........ 82  C2
Fenagh Leitrm ........... 87  E2
Ferbane Offaly............ 84  C2
Fermoy Cork............... 83  E2
Ferns Wexfd............... 85  E3
Fethard Tippry ........... 84  C3
Fethard Wexfd ........... 85  D4
Fintona F & O............. 88  C3
Fivemiletown
    M Ulst.................... 88  C3
Foxford Mayo............. 86  C2
Freemount Cork ........ 83  D2

## G

Galbally Limrck .......... 83  E2
Galway C Gal .............. 86  C3
Garrison F & O ........... 87  D1
Garvagh CC & G ......... 89  D2
Gilford AB & C ............ 89  D3
Glaslough Monhan..... 88  C3
Gleann Cholm Cille
    Donegl ................... 88  A2
Glenamaddy
    Galway .................. 87  D3
Glenarm E Antr .......... 89  E2
Glenavy L & C ............ 89  D3
Glenbeigh Kerry......... 82  B3
Glencolumbkille
    Donegl ................... 88  A2
Glengarriff Cork ......... 82  C3
Glenties Donegl ......... 88  B2
Glin Limrck................. 82  C2
Golden Tippry............. 84  B3
Goresbridge Kilken..... 85  D3
Gorey Wexfd .............. 85  E3
Gort Galway ............... 86  C4
Gortin F & O ............... 88  C2
Gowran Kilken............ 85  D3
Graiguenamanagh
    Kilken .................... 85  D3

Granard Longfd.......... 88  C4
Grange Sligo .............. 87  D1
Greencastle Donegl.... 88  C1
Greencastle F & O ...... 88  C2
Greenore Louth.......... 89  D4
Greyabbey A & ND ..... 89  E3
Greystones Wicklw..... 85  E2
Gulladuff M Ulst......... 89  D2

## H

Hacketstown
    Carlow ................... 85  D3
Headford Galway........ 86  C3
Hilltown NM & D........ 89  D3
Holywood A & ND ...... 89  E2
Hospital Limrck .......... 83  D2
Howth Dublin ............ 85  E1

## I

Inagh Clare................. 82  C1
Inch Kerry .................. 82  B2
Inishcrone Sligo......... 86  C1
Innishannon Cork ...... 83  D3
Irvinestown F & O....... 88  B3

## J

Johnstown Kilken...... 84  C3

## K

Kanturk Cork.............. 83  D2
Keadue Roscom ......... 87  D2
Keady AB & C ............. 89  D3
Kealkill Cork............... 82  C3
Keel Mayo.................. 86  B2
Kells Meath................ 85  D1
Kenmare Kerry ........... 82  C3
Kesh F & O ................. 88  B3
Kilbeggan Wmeath .... 84  C2
Kilcar Donegl............. 88  A2
Kilcock Meath ............ 85  D1
Kilcoole Wicklw.......... 85  E2
Kilcormac Offaly ........ 84  C2
Kilcullen Kildre........... 85  D2
Kildare Kildre............. 85  D2
Kilfenora Clare........... 86  C4
Kilgarvan Kerry........... 82  C3
Kilkee Clare ............... 82  C1
Kilkeel NM & D .......... 89  E4
Kilkenny Kilken .......... 84  C3
Kill Kildre................... 85  D2
Kill Watfd................... 84  C4
Killala Mayo............... 86  C1
Killaloe Clare.............. 83  D1
Killarney Kerry ........... 82  C3
Killashandra Cavan .... 88  C4
Killenaule Tippry ........ 84  C3
Killorglin Kerry........... 82  C2
Killucan Wmeath ....... 85  D1
Killurin Offaly............. 84  C2
Killybegs Donegl ....... 88  A2
Killyleagh NM & D ...... 89  E3
Kilmacanogue
    Wicklw ................... 85  E2
Kilmacthomas
    Watfd .................... 84  C4
Kilmaganny Kilken ..... 84  C3
Kilmaine Mayo ........... 86  C2
Kilmallock Limrck ...... 83  D2

Kilmanagh Kilken ...... 84  C3
Kilmihil Clare............. 82  C1
Kilmore Quay
    Wexfd .................... 85  D4
Kilmuckridge
    Wexfd .................... 85  E3
Kilpedder Wicklw........ 85  E2
Kilrea CC & G ............. 89  D2
Kilrush Clare.............. 82  C1
Kilsheelan Tippry ....... 84  C4
Kiltimagh Mayo ......... 86  C2
Kilworth Cork ............ 83  E2
Kingscourt Cavan ...... 89  D4
Kinlough Leitrm......... 87  D1
Kinnegad Meath......... 85  D1
Kinnitty Offaly............ 84  C2
Kinsale Cork............... 83  D3
Kinvara Galway .......... 86  C4
Kircubbin A & ND ...... 89  E3
Knock Mayo ............... 86  C2
Knockcroghery
    Roscom.................. 87  D3

## L

Lanesborough
    Longfd ................... 84  B1
Laragh Wicklw ........... 85  E2
Larne E Antr .............. 89  E2
Lauragh Kerry ............ 82  C3
Leap Cork .................. 82  C4
Leenaun Galway ........ 86  B3
Leighlinbridge
    Carlow ................... 85  D3
Leixlip Kildre ............. 85  D2
Letterfrack
    Galway .................. 86  B3
Letterkenny
    Donegl ................... 88  B2
Lifford Donegl............ 88  C2
Limavady CC & G ....... 88  C2
Limerick Limrck ......... 83  D1
Lisbellaw F & O .......... 88  C3
Lisburn L & C ............. 89  D3
Lisdoonvarna Clare..... 86  C4
Lismore Watfd ........... 84  C4
Lisnaskea F & O ......... 88  C3
Listowel Kerry ........... 82  C2
Londonderry
    D & S ..................... 88  C2
Longford Longfd......... 84  C1
Longwood Meath....... 85  D1
Loughbrickland
    AB & C ................... 89  D3
Loughglinn
    Roscom.................. 87  D2
Loughrea Galway ....... 87  D4
Louisburgh Mayo ....... 86  B2
Lucan Dublin ............. 85  E2
Lurgan AB & C ........... 89  D3
Lusk Dublin ............... 85  E1

## M

Macroom Cork............ 83  D3
Maghera M Ulst......... 89  D2
Magherafelt M Ulst.... 89  D2
Maguiresbridge
    F & O ..................... 88  C3
Maigh Cuilinn
    Galway .................. 86  C3
Malahide Dublin ........ 85  E1
Málainn Mhóir
    Donegl ................... 88  A2

Malin Donegl ............... 88 C1
Malin More Donegl .... 88 A2
Mallow Cork ................ 83 D2
Manorhamilton
   Leitrm ...................... 87 D1
Markethill AB & C ...... 89 D3
Maynooth Kildre ........ 85 D1
Mayobridge
   NM & D ..................... 89 D3
Midleton Cork ............. 83 E3
Milford Donegl ........... 88 B2
Millstreet Cork ........... 83 D3
Miltown Malbay
   Clare ......................... 82 C1
Mitchelstown
   Cork .......................... 83 E2
Moate Wmeath ........... 84 C1
Mohill Leitrm .............. 87 E2
Monaghan Monhan ... 88 C3
Monasterevin
   Kildre ........................ 85 D2
Moneymore M Ulst .... 89 D2
Mooncoin Kilken ........ 84 C4
Mountbellew
   Galway ...................... 87 D3
Mountmellick
   Laois ......................... 84 C2
Mountrath Laois ......... 84 C2
Moville Donegl ........... 88 C1
Moy M Ulst .................. 89 D3
Moycullen Galway ...... 86 C3
Mucklagh Offaly ......... 84 C2
Muff Donegl ................ 88 C2
Muine Bheag
   Carlow ...................... 85 D3
Mullagh Cavan ........... 88 C4
Mullaghmore Sligo ..... 87 D1
Mullinahone Tippry ... 84 C3
Mullingar Wmeath ..... 84 C1
Mulranny Mayo .......... 86 B2
Murrisk Mayo .............. 86 B2
Murroe Limrck ............ 83 D1

**N**

Naas Kildre .................. 85 D2
Naul Dublin ................. 85 E1
Navan Meath ............... 85 D1
Nenagh Tippry ............ 83 E1
Newbawn Wexfd ......... 85 D4
Newbliss Monhan ....... 88 C3
Newbridge Kildre ....... 85 D2
Newcastle NM & D ..... 89 E3
Newcastle Wicklw ...... 85 E2
Newcastle West
   Limrck ...................... 83 D2
Newmarket Cork ........ 83 D2
Newmarket-on-
   Fergus Clare ............ 83 D1
Newport Mayo ............ 86 B2
Newport Tippry .......... 83 D1
New Ross Wexfd ......... 85 D4
Newry NM & D ............ 89 D3
Newtownabbey
   A & N ........................ 89 E2
Newtownards
   A & ND ...................... 89 E3
Newtownbutler
   F & O ........................ 88 C3
Newtowncunningham
   Donegl ...................... 88 C2
Newtownforbes
   Longfd ...................... 84 C1
Newtownhamilton
   NM & D ..................... 89 D3

Newtownmountkennedy
   Wicklw ...................... 85 E2
Newtownstewart
   D & S ........................ 88 C2

**O**

Oldcastle Meath ......... 88 C4
Omagh F & O ............... 88 C3
Oranmore Galway ...... 86 C3
Oughterard Galway .... 86 C3

**P**

Pallas Green Limrck ... 83 E2
Partry Mayo ................ 86 C2
Passage East Watfd ... 85 D4
Passage West Cork .... 83 E3
Patrickswell Limrck ... 83 D1
Pettigo Donegl ........... 88 B3
Piltown Kilken ............ 84 C4
Plumbridge D & S ...... 88 C2
Pomeroy M Ulst .......... 88 C3
Portadown AB & C ..... 89 D3
Portaferry A & ND ..... 89 E3
Portarlington Laois .... 85 D2
Portavogie A & ND ..... 89 E3
Portglenone E Antr .... 89 D2
Port Laoise Laois ....... 84 C2
Portlaw Watfd ............. 84 C4
Portmagee Kerry ........ 82 B3
Portmarnock Dublin .. 85 E1
Portnoo Donegl .......... 88 A2
Portrush CC & G ........ 89 D1
Portstewart CC & G .. 89 D1
Portumna Galway ...... 87 D4
Poyntzpass AB & C .... 89 D3
Prosperous Kildre ...... 85 D2

**Q**

Quin Clare .................. 83 D1

**R**

Ramelton Donegl ....... 88 B2
Randalstown
   A & N ........................ 89 D2
Raphoe Donegl ........... 88 B2
Rasharkin CC & G ...... 89 D2
Rathangan Kildre ....... 85 D2
Rathcoole Dublin ....... 85 E2
Rathcormac Cork ....... 83 E3
Rathdowney Laois ..... 84 C3
Rathdrum Wicklw ...... 85 E2
Rathfriland AB & C .... 89 D3
Rathkeale Limrck ....... 83 D2
Ráth Luirc Cork .......... 83 D2
Rathmore Kerry ......... 82 C3
Rathmullan Donegl ... 88 C1
Rathnew Wicklw ......... 85 E2
Rathvilly Carlow ........ 85 D3
Ratoath Meath ........... 85 E1
Recess Galway ........... 86 B3
Rhode Offaly ............... 85 D2
Ringaskiddy Cork ....... 83 E3
Riverstick Cork .......... 83 D3
Rochfortbridge
   Wmeath .................... 84 C1
Rockcorry Monhan .... 88 C4
Roscommon
   Roscom ..................... 87 D3

Roscrea Tippry ........... 84 C2
Rosscarbery Cork ...... 83 D4
Rosses Point Sligo ..... 87 D1
Rosslare Wexfd .......... 85 E4
Rosslare Harbour
   Wexfd ....................... 85 E4
Rosslea F & O ............. 88 C3
Rossnowlagh
   Donegl ...................... 88 B3
Rostrevor NM & D ..... 89 D4
Roundstone Galway ... 86 B3
Roundwood Wicklw ... 85 E2
Rush Dublin ................ 85 E1

**S**

Saintfield NM & D ..... 89 E3
Sallins Kildre ............. 85 D2
Scarriff Clare .............. 87 D4
Schull Cork ................. 82 C4
Seskinore F & O ......... 88 C3
Shannon Clare ........... 83 D1
Shannonbridge
   Offaly ....................... 87 D3
Shercock Cavan .......... 88 C4
Shillelagh Wicklw ...... 85 D3
Silvermines Tippry .... 83 E1
Sion Mills D & S ......... 88 C2
Sixmilebridge
   Clare ......................... 83 D1
Skerries Dublin .......... 85 E1
Skibbereen Cork ........ 82 C4
Slane Meath ............... 85 D1
Sligo Sligo .................. 87 D1
Sneem Kerry ............... 82 B3
Spanish Point
   Clare ......................... 82 C1
Spiddal Galway .......... 86 C3
Sraith Salach
   Galway ...................... 86 B3
Stewartstown
   M Ulst ....................... 89 D3
Strabane D & S ........... 88 C2
Stradbally Laois ......... 85 D2
Strandhill Sligo .......... 87 D1
Stranorlar Donegl ...... 88 B2
Strokestown
   Roscom ..................... 87 D2
Summerhill Meath ..... 85 D1
Swan Laois .................. 85 D3
Swanlinbar Cavan ..... 88 B3
Swinford Mayo ........... 86 C2
Swords Dublin ............ 85 E1

**T**

Taghmon Wexfd ......... 85 D4
Tallaght Dublin .......... 85 E2
Tallow Watfd ............... 83 E3
Tandragee
   AB & C ...................... 89 D3
Tarbert Kerry ............. 82 C1
Templemore
   Tippry ....................... 84 C3
Termonfeckin
   Louth ........................ 89 D4
Thomastown
   Kilken ....................... 85 D3
Thurles Tippry ........... 84 C3
Timoleague Cork ........ 83 D3
Tinahely Wicklw ......... 85 E3
Tipperary Tippry ....... 84 B3
Tobercurry Sligo ........ 87 D2
Tobermore M Ulst ...... 89 D2

Toomevara
   Tippry ....................... 84 B3
Toormore Cork ........... 82 C4
Tower Cork .................. 83 D3
Tralee Kerry ............... 82 C2
Tramore Watfd ........... 85 D4
Trim Meath ................. 85 D1
Tuam Galway .............. 86 C3
Tubbercurry Sligo ...... 87 D2
Tulla Clare .................. 83 D1
Tullamore Offaly ........ 84 C2
Tullow Carlow ............ 85 D3
Tulsk Roscom ............. 87 D2
Turlough Mayo ........... 86 C2

**U**

Urlingford Kilken ....... 84 C3

**V**

Virginia Cavan ............ 88 C4

**W**

Warrenpoint
   NM & D ..................... 89 D4
Waterford Watfd ........ 85 D4
Watergrasshill Cork ... 83 E3
Waterville Kerry ........ 82 B3
Wellingtonbridge
   Wexfd ....................... 85 D4
Westport Mayo ........... 86 C2
Wexford Wexfd ........... 85 E4
Whitegate Cork .......... 83 E3
Whitehead E Antr ...... 89 E2
Wicklow Wicklw ......... 85 E2
Woodenbridge
   Wicklw ...................... 85 E3
Woodford Galway ...... 87 D4

**Y**

Youghal Cork .............. 83 E3